Post-Crisis Leadership

Post-Crisis Leadership

Resilience, Renewal, and Reinvention in the Aftermath of Disruption

RALPH A. GIGLIOTTI

Rutgers University Press

New Brunswick, Camden, and Newark, New Jersey,
London and Oxford

Rutgers University Press is a department of Rutgers,
The State University of New Jersey, one of the leading public
research universities in the nation. By publishing worldwide,
it furthers the University's mission of dedication to excellence
in teaching, scholarship, research, and clinical care.

Library of Congress Cataloging-in-Publication Data

Names: Gigliotti, Ralph A., author.
Title: Post-crisis leadership : resilience, renewal, and reinvention in the
aftermath of disruption / Ralph A. Gigliotti.
Description: New Brunswick, New Jersey : Rutgers University Press, 2025. |
Includes bibliographical references and index.
Identifiers: LCCN 2024003745 | ISBN 9781978838482 (paperback) |
ISBN 9781978838499 (hardcover) | ISBN 9781978838505 (epub) |
ISBN 9781978838512 (pdf)
Subjects: LCSH: Education, Higher—United States—Administration. |
Crisis management—United States. | Universities and colleges—United
States—Administration. | Educational leadership—United States. |
Communication in higher education—United States.
Classification: LCC LB2341 .G487 2024 | DDC 378.1/01—dc23/eng/20240215
LC record available at https://lccn.loc.gov/2024003745

A British Cataloging-in-Publication record for this book is available
from the British Library.

References to internet websites (URLs) were accurate at the time of writing. Neither
the author nor Rutgers University Press is responsible for URLs that may have
expired or changed since the manuscript was prepared.

∞ The paper used in this publication meets the requirements of the American
National Standard for Information Sciences—Permanence of Paper for Printed
Library Materials, ANSI Z39.48-1992.

rutgersuniversitypress.org

In memory of my mother, Gabriella Gigliotti (1960–2022), who inspired me to dream big, work hard, love unconditionally, and find meaning, healing, and growth in times of distress.

Contents

Preface

In the depths of crisis, individuals and the organizations to which they belong experience disruption—a disruption from what they have come to expect and accept as normal; a disruption of a shared set of principles or values; or a disruption of their safety, well-being, and sense of connection to others. If we take as a point of reference any event or situation that is commonly viewed as a crisis—natural disasters, acts of violence, periods of financial turmoil, or a global pandemic—time and time again we bear witness to a foreseeable sequence that includes the onset of a predicted or sudden disruption, a collective search for information and answers, a period of prolonged media attention, and an expectation of scripted responses from leaders of the organization or community impacted by the incident. The life cycle of a crisis typically evolves through the stages of pre-crisis, crisis, and post-crisis, with much of the scholarly and professional literature focused on the requisite preparation prior to the crisis and the details of what happens (or fails to happen) during the event. The emphasis on the pre-crisis and crisis phases is understandable given the criticality of prevention, management, communication, and coordination during these phases. Crises are provocative—they can garner national and international attention, romanticize organizational heroes, and illuminate the dark side of organizational life. And, as we have come to experience, fear, danger, and uncertainty often accompany these critical incidents.

A number of authors focus on the ways in which organizations and communities come together in the aftermath of crisis—a disaster collectivism characterized by "the sense of immersion in the moment and solidarity with others caused by the rupture in everyday life, an emotion graver than happiness but deeply positive" (Solnit, 2010, p. 5). This idea reflects to some degree the growing emphasis on resilience studies in disaster research (Fritz, 1961/1996; Perry & Quarantelli, 2005; Quarantelli, 1998), communication studies (Buzzanell, 2010; Chewning et al., 2013; Doerfel et al., 2010), and psychology (Bonanno, 2004; Bonanno et al., 2011; D. Fletcher & Sarkar, 2013; Richardson, 2002). Less attention is given to the actions, responsibilities, and expectations of those engaged in post-crisis leadership and the ways in which leadership practices can accelerate or decelerate the recovery and renewal processes. *Post-Crisis Leadership* provides a framework for leaders who are responsible for navigating this post-crisis stage—a stage that is not easily demarcated from the first two, one that lacks the studied best practices found in much of the crisis and risk management literature, and one that remains a source of widespread scrutiny from those most directly impacted by the incident in question.

I began preparing this book in the midst of the COVID-19 pandemic—a once-in-a-century public health crisis that ravaged communities across the globe and accelerated widespread change for institutions of all kinds. The pandemic contributed to the closure of roughly two hundred thousand establishments in the United States, and the sudden shift to a fully online environment has led many organizations to rethink the nature of in-person work. Although the acute nature of this crisis continues to recede from memory, we find ourselves in a moment in time that is marked by a growing commentary on the individual awakening and collective renaissance that is made possible during this post-pandemic period.

In addition to responding to and recovering from the widespread yet disproportionate impact of the pandemic, we remain in the midst of converging challenges nationally and globally, including racial injustice; climate change; economic inflation;

the spread of disinformation and misinformation, political polarization, and ongoing threats to democracy; an increase in individuals reporting symptoms of anxiety or depression; the outbreak of war in various parts of the world; and an increase in gun violence and violent crime. These divisive issues, along with many others, create a barrier that stands in the way of mutual understanding, stalls individual and collective healing, and will likely influence the strategic trajectory of organizations as we imagine our shared future.

In the midst of what has been characterized as the Great Resignation, the Great Reshuffle, the Great Attrition, and the Great Discontent, people are leaving their jobs at a record pace in search of more money, more flexibility, and more fulfillment. According to one Gallup report, 51 percent of America's working population is actively job searching or seeking other opportunities (Mosser, 2023). The U.S. Bureau of Labor Statistics reports that more than 47 million people quit their jobs over the course of 2021, representing 23 percent of the total U.S. workforce. No organization is immune from this profound change in the labor market, and as supported by a growing body of research, organizations that are expected to thrive in this environment are those who privilege purpose, engagement, and a culture that celebrates diversity, inclusion, and belonging.

Colleges and universities continue to navigate the complexities of this contemporary moment. Institutions of higher education, among the first to shift to entirely online operations during the pandemic, must now consider how best to respond to the demands of a post-pandemic environment. Because of the many intersecting challenges ranging from climate change to the erosion of civil discourse, colleges and universities occupy a central role in both the study of these issues and the institutional reaction to them. And in response to the waves of change in the labor market, there is a noticeable increase in attention to issues related to faculty and staff disengagement (McClure & Fryar, 2022), with colleges and universities reporting similar hiring and retention challenges as other employers. As documented in a College and University Professional Association for Human Resources (2022) report, institutions of higher education are experiencing a decline in full-time and part-time staff as well as tenure-track faculty, in addition to failing to provide pay increases to keep pace with growing inflation. Additionally, as part of this shifting landscape, colleges and universities are experiencing a decline in public trust and an increase in financial pressures that pose a threat to their viability.

As we peer into a post-pandemic future—one that will involve a recalibration of culture, strategy, and the employee value proposition across organizations—the moment demands a consideration of the dynamics of post-crisis leadership.

Some specific questions guiding this scholarly inquiry include the following:

- How can leaders distinguish the crisis from the post-crisis phases, and what does this distinction mean for the practice of leadership?
- In what ways can leaders contribute to the conditions associated with organizational learning, healing, and renewal in the aftermath of crisis?
- How can the pursuit of strategic reinvention help an organization to move forward with purpose and clarity, and what risks might emerge if these efforts are perceived by others to be hurried, insensitive, or grounded in faulty assumptions?
- How might those engaged in leadership and followership collectively encounter and co-create meaning and growth in the collective transition from crisis to post-crisis?
- Last, given the distinct and at times competing expectations of different stakeholders who are often disproportionately impacted by crises, how might leaders navigate situations where some remain immersed in crisis and others long to move forward?

In an effort to answer these questions, I will draw upon various streams of interdisciplinary research along with examples and stories from across the higher education landscape in the design of a communication-informed framework for values-based post-crisis leadership.

Given the scarcity of scholarly and professional writing on post-crisis leadership, and in recognition of the various environmental factors that weigh heavily on organizations of all kinds, this book is meant to inspire reflection and encourage intentionality among those engaged in leadership during this historical moment.

I continue to believe that it is in the darkness and chaos of crisis where values-based leadership becomes most critical, most visible, and most desired (Gigliotti, 2019). And, by extending values-based leadership as a guide during this transition from crisis to post-crisis, learning, healing, growth, and transformation become possible. Effective leadership in the aftermath of crisis can stimulate meaning-making, inspire reinvention, and bring about renewal.

Through my various roles working in university strategy and academic leadership development at a prominent public research university, in addition to the many conversations I have engaged in with colleagues from across sectors, I have been struck by the following observations, each of which will be disentangled and explored in richer detail throughout this book:

- Crisis leadership—which takes account of leading before, during, *and* after crisis—is an imperative for leaders at all levels.
- The complexities of leading in and through crisis can contribute to the absence of attention given to post-crisis leadership. The fatigue, frustration, and even trauma present in times of crisis have the potential to stall the healing and recovery that could result post-crisis. Often relegated as an afterthought in crisis scholarship and practice, the ability to navigate the post-crisis period can distinguish highly effective leaders and organizations.
- An investment in post-crisis leadership development—along with an investment in organizational recovery and learning during this period—serves both short-term and long-term interests, while helping to build capacity in responding to the inevitable crises that have yet to occur.

- Internal and external stakeholders impacted by crises crave hope, compassion, and trust—and engaging these audiences in co-creating a path forward can cultivate resilience and renewal, focusing on both a return to what was and a pivot to what might have never been.
- With an underlying commitment to values-based, principle-oriented, and people-centered practices, these five leadership practices stand out as especially critical in the aftermath of crisis: (1) encourage learning, (2) inspire growth, (3) stimulate meaning-making, (4) pursue reinvention, and (5) advance renewal.
- Communication serves a critical role in each of the various dimensions of post-crisis leadership, and a communication orientation can help us to better understand the paradoxes, processes, and patterns that arise during these periods of immense tension and, at times, transcendence.

Road Map for This Book

I wrote this book with multiple audiences in mind: organizational leaders and leadership teams seeking to strengthen their effectiveness in moving beyond the challenges of our time; scholars and practitioners hoping to deepen their understanding of post-crisis leadership concepts and strategies; undergraduate and graduate students across academic disciplines who are studying the intersection of crisis, leadership, communication, strategy, and organizational development; and those engaged in the design and facilitation of training and development programs preparing current and future leaders to navigate critical incidents and the periods following these incidents with care, compassion, and civility.

Each of the chapters includes a summary of the relevant interdisciplinary literature, examples of post-crisis leadership from across colleges and universities, and a list of implications for practice and key questions based on the chapter's theme. For readers seeking applied strategies for navigating this post-crisis period, the concluding considerations for post-crisis leadership action may serve as a useful guide for theory-informed practice. It is my hope that by taking the time to engage in thoughtful reflection regarding the content and questions introduced in this text, readers will approach the critical period following crisis with greater intentionality and sense of purpose.

The book begins with a summary of key terms, concepts, and conceptual underpinnings. Specifically, we will spend time reviewing the meaning of crisis and crisis leadership, along with the dynamics of leadership communication that come into play during the various stages of the crisis life cycle. With an emphasis on values-based leadership, chapter 1 introduces a model for post-crisis leadership that serves as a framework for the remainder of the book. Each of the subsequent chapters explores the various components of the framework for post-crisis leadership, with a focus on learning, growth, meaning-making, reinvention, and renewal. The book concludes with a slate of recommended strategies for those engaged in leadership in the aftermath of crisis, along with considerations for future scholarship on this subject.

During a period of prolonged disruption, uncertainty, and loss, there is often a collective longing for hope, healing, and transcendence. This book contributes to this important moment, and the concepts, stories, and strategies shared herein aim to advance the theory and practice of post-crisis leadership in ways that I hope will offer insight and inspiration.

Post-Crisis Leadership

Introduction

Contemporary Crisis Conditions and Theoretical Underpinnings for Post-Crisis Leadership

Crises represent turning points for organizations, communities, and the individuals who make up these collective entities. They serve as distinct moments in time that are often accompanied by fear and the potential for change and transformation. Drawing upon its etymological roots, the word "crisis" originally referred to a "turning point," similar to the medical usage of the term in Latin to imply the turning point of an illness (Ulmer et al., 2022). Or, as Fink (1986) posits, a crisis represents a "turning point, not necessarily laden with irreparable negativity but rather characterized by a certain degree of risk and uncertainty" (p. 23). Ulmer et al. (2022) draw attention to the Chinese word for crisis, *wei chi*, which signifies a dangerous opportunity. Indeed, crises have the potential to disrupt and destroy operations, endanger and enthrall individuals, and mobilize and motivate individual and collective change. The perilous conditions of crisis may invoke fear and frustration, while also serving as "necessary correctives" in revealing what was broken and in need of improvement prior to the incident. At their core, crises have the potential to uproot and existentially threaten the work of an organization, leading Seeger and Ulmer (2001) to describe these moments as "high impact events that often strip an organization to its core values" (p. 374).

This introduction will provide a point of entry into the study of crisis and crisis leadership in higher education and will propose a model for values-based post-crisis leadership that lies at the core of this book.

Conceptualizing Contemporary Crises

The conditions of the current historical moment contribute to what some might characterize as a collective inflection point—a point in time marked by tremendous disagreement, discord, and disruption. In response to many of the challenges and pressures posed in the preface, organizations of all kinds—public and private, nonprofit and for-profit, old and new—face a world that looks different in many ways to the world pre-COVID-19. Although many aspects of our lives returned to "normal" as public health conditions improved, the experience of living, working, and leading through a pandemic—and for some, the loss that accompanied this public health crisis—has the potential to alter both our individual and collective mindset. This shift in mindset echoes the shift that was already underway in the contemporary workplace prior to the pandemic, with the public health crisis both accelerating and intensifying this transformation. As Gallup researchers note, the workplace of the past required a focus on paycheck, workplace satisfaction, and job security, with managers often responsible for conducting annual reviews that tended to center on areas for employee improvement (Clifton & Harter, 2019). The shift in workplace expectations places a prominent emphasis on purpose, development, and work-life integration, with managers playing active roles as coaches who are engaged in ongoing, frequent, and future-oriented conversations that reflect the unique talents of each employee. In addition to this shift in workplace expectations, the prolonged disruption that has occurred in recent years has led many to revisit their core purpose—what is our "why" for engaging in our work; what are the deeper intentions for which we strive; and what are the problems, questions, and issues calling for our attention?

For both individuals and collective entities, including work groups, teams, organizations, communities, and societies, this inflection point eventually may be punctuated into a before and an after—pre- and post-COVID-19—but a broader historical lens allows us to take account of the echoes of past inflection points facing the higher education sector. As Birnbaum and Shushok (2001) suggest, "Crisis is related to change, and change always seems to be more rapid in the contemporary era than in our memories of the past. But the immediacy of the present always leads us to feel under pressure from what we believed to be an increased pace of change" (p. 71). The arc of history for colleges and universities in the United States, for example, is full of local, national, and global crises that served as catalysts for change in the post-secondary education system (Thelin, 2019). Writing specifically about the dramatic change that occurred during the Industrial Revolution, Levine and Van Pelt (2021) detail seven overlapping stages and argue that the current transformation of higher education might follow a similar pattern: (1) demand for change; (2) denial of the need to change; (3) experimentation and reform initiatives with a focus on attempting to repair the existing model of higher education; (4) the establishment of new models of higher education at the periphery rather than the mainstream of the enterprise that sought to replace the existing model rather than repair it; (5) diffusion of the new models with a prestigious institution at the center, leading the effort and other mainstream institutions adopting the changes in their own ways; (6) standardizing the cornucopia of varying practices and policies that diffusion spawned; and (7) scaling up and integrating the various pieces of standardized practice and policy to create the industrial system of higher education (p. 104). As the authors go on to note, and as will be detailed further in chapter 4 on the subject of post-crisis reinvention, "Higher education continues in its schizophrenic role of both opposing and experimenting with change in the early stages of the transformation" (p. 108).

These observations highlight several relevant factors for how we might study the exigencies of the current moment. First, we find ourselves at an important historical juncture—one that is punctuated by a global pandemic, national racial reckoning, spreading international conflict, and increased damage and destruction that is the result of human-induced climate change—and there is a widespread recognition of the crisis-like conditions that represent this moment in time. Second, the "look backward" (Levine & Van Pelt, 2021) and the use of a broader historical lens allow us to consider the linkages to earlier periods of transformation and to recognize the ways in which the echoes of the past might inform how we come to understand the conditions of the present. Finally, despite the tremendous harm, loss, and turmoil faced by many at this time, the current converging disruptions have had a disproportionate impact on various individuals and groups, and what may be a crisis of catastrophic magnitude for so many—particularly those who have encountered loss of homes, livelihoods, or loved ones—may be viewed by others as an opportunity—an opportunity for individual and collective reinvention, an opportunity for more flexible work arrangements or broadened job prospects, or an opportunity to spend more time at home with family or friends. As supported by the growing research on the subject of leadership generativity, living systems adapt and evolve in response to information, feedback, and external cues—and despite the danger, fear, and loss that might accompany crises, these critical incidents also provide unique opportunities for growth, learning, renewal, and generosity (Allen, 2018; Devies & Guthrie, 2024; Gigliotti, 2024).

Yet, what might happen if we call into question the very existence of crisis? Spector (2020) goes so far as to suggest that there is no such thing as a crisis, at least not "a corporeal thing" or "object that can be placed under a microscope, manipulated, examined, and experimented on" (p. 304). Rather, as he argues in his book *Constructing Crisis: Leaders, Crisis, and Claims of Urgency*, crisis is "a label, a claim of urgency employed, typically by leaders, to characterize a set of contingencies that are, together, taken to pose a serious and immediate threat" (p. 304). As Birnbaum and Shushok (2001) suggest, "The strong rhetoric and vivid imageries of crisis are useful tools with which to gain attention, power, and control of organizational and symbolic processes in a noisy world" (pp. 69, 70). Crises are socially constructed, and we might modify our inquiry to explore the question of a crisis *for whom* (Gigliotti, 2020a). Who has authority to label an event or series of events as a crisis? For the formal leader, in what ways does the invocation of crisis allow one to expedite decision making, sidestep formal lines of decision making, or otherwise behave in ways that might not be tolerated by members of the organization? For the individual or groups of individuals who lack formal authority, in what ways might the invocation of crisis bring attention to issues that might otherwise be treated with less seriousness or less urgency? Rather than treat crises solely as external phenomena imposed from the outside—think of the hurricane that makes landfall, causing widespread physical destruction, or the active shooter whose actions lead to loss of life—we might also explore the ways in which crises are socially constructed and the ways in which the invocation of crisis creates opportunities for action and attention that otherwise might not be possible.

I would like to offer the following working definition of *crises*, with an acknowledgment of the inherent degree of subjectivity involved in the naming and labeling of a crisis: "Crises are events or situations of significant magnitude that threaten reputations, impact the lives of those involved in the institution, disrupt the ways in which the organization functions, have a cascading influence on leadership responsibilities and obligations across units/divisions, and require an immediate response from leaders" (Gigliotti, 2019, p. 61).

Any number of events or situations could meet this broad definition, and in some cases, certain types of crises are unique to one's sector or industry. For example, the seminal case involving cyanide-laced capsules of Extra-Strength Tylenol in 1982 became a defining crisis for health-care and pharmaceutical giant Johnson & Johnson, whereas allegations of research misconduct, issues related to student mental health, or an athletic hazing scandal might be most germane within the education sector. Yet, there are some examples of crises that cut across sectors and industries, such as natural disasters, cyberattacks, active shooter situations, or incidents of high-profile workplace harassment.

In considering the types of crises one might encounter in their organization, Coombs (2022) provides a useful framework organized by degree of responsibility. In some situations, the organization is a victim in the case of the crisis, such as during natural disasters, rumors, workplace violence, and product tampering/malevolence. Coombs gathers this set of crises into what he calls a "victim cluster." For a second set of crises, what he labels the "accidental cluster," the organization maintains low crisis responsibility, and these might include challenges, technical-error accidents, and technical-error product harm. Coombs's final set of crises form the "preventable cluster," for which the organization is highly culpable, including human-error accidents, human-error product harm, and organizational misdeeds.

Writing specifically about the higher education context, Birnbaum and Shushok (2001) differentiate four types of institutional crises:

- Pandemic crisis: A crisis that is claimed continuously and with great frequency.
- Chronic crisis: A crisis that appears with moderate continuity and frequency.
- Sporadic crisis: A crisis that represents a response to transient social conditions and that is not expected to be cited with much frequency as a major concern in the future.
- Idiosyncratic crisis: A crisis that represents the views of small, specialized constituencies on issues seen by others as relatively unimportant. (p. 64)

In addition to classifying and categorizing crises based on type, degree of responsibility, or frequency, we also know that crises are likely to move through some predictable life cycle. Although no two crises are the same (Gigliotti & O'Dowd, 2021), these events and situations can be separated into pre-crisis, crisis, and post-crisis phases. Most crises tend to progress through these distinct phases, although the boundaries of the phases often become better defined and more coherent retrospectively as we look back and consider the broader arc of the event or series of events. The writing on exemplary practices during the pre-crisis and crisis phases is expansive, and many of these practices are well documented in the scholarly and professional literature (Seeger, 2006). For example, during the pre-crisis stage, there is an emphasis on planning and preparation. Leadership teams might use this time to review plans and protocols; form and prepare emergency management teams; scan the horizon; and routinely test their responses through simulations, drills, and case studies. Once an acute crisis strikes, communication is paramount, particularly in responding quickly, confidently, and in ways that reflect and reinforce the values of the organization. Other well-documented leadership recommendations during this time involve the importance of demonstrating presence, availability, transparency, consistency, and honesty in the midst of disruption. Finally, much of the crisis literature addresses the imperative for leaders to triage immediate needs while also responding in ways that strategically position the organization for the future—in essence, negotiating and straddling both the present and future time horizons, all the while leaning upon the unique histories, traditions, and expectations of the past.

As well as recognizing the subjectivity of crisis, we need to acknowledge that the phases through which these events progress are also inherently subjective—and the boundaries between pre-crisis, crisis, and post-crisis may be better understood as curtains than walls. If we take the COVID-19 pandemic as an example, for many institutions throughout the United States, March and April 2020 may be regarded as the period of acute crisis in quickly shifting to a fully remote work environment and in adapting operations, policies, and procedures based on the shifting public health guidelines at the time. For individuals and organizations with clinical responsibilities, the months that followed the onset of the pandemic may be viewed as a period of prolonged crisis, which included responding to the surge in emergency room visits, followed by localized waves of increased hospitalizations. For those in educational settings, the evolution of public health guidelines in spring 2020, the 2020–2021 academic year, and the 2021–2022 academic year contributed to continuously changing crisis leadership responsibilities, expectations, and challenges. And for those in the public and private sectors, the needs of constituents, local businesses, and multinational organizations evolved during the life cycle of the pandemic. This in turn led to various points of crisis depending on the scope of impact, the types of products and services offered, and the ability of businesses, for example, to pivot effectively to changing environmental conditions. At the time of this writing, many are looking past the crises of 2020–2023 (post-crisis) and preparing for what might come next (pre-crisis), all while responding to the longer-term changes and challenges that are in some ways related to this period of prolonged disruption. Viewed as curtains and not rigid walls, the components, characteristics, and conditions of the pre-crisis, crisis, and post-crisis phases bleed into one another and we can often peer beyond the curtain to see (or, more often, speculate) what remains behind and what might lie ahead. It is incumbent on those engaged in leadership to adequately diagnose where in the crisis life cycle the organization might be and also to recognize and respond to the individualized needs of those they lead—some of whom may be situated at different points in the continuum.

In this book, I am interested in focusing on what happens—or in some cases, what fails to happen—in the days, weeks, and months following the onset of the crisis. As the dust settles, as communities rebuild, and as individuals begin to reorient themselves around who they are and who they want to be in the aftermath of crisis, this period serves as an important moment for reflection, reinvention, and renewal. The post-crisis period is a pronounced juncture for individual and collective meaning-making, and communication plays a critical role in how individuals and organizations come together, heal, and move forward during this time. For those engaged in formal and informal leadership following a crisis, and those seeking to exercise leadership in the aftermath of a crisis, there is an opportunity to learn from the disruptions of this historic period as we advance the study and practice of post-crisis leadership.

Crises—or events of significant magnitude that are perceived by some or many to be crises—will continue to impact individuals, organizations, and societies, and perhaps with increased frequency and damage. The model presented in this chapter offers a way of thinking about values-based crisis leadership in the aftermath of disruption, and it can also help to differentiate effective leaders and organizations from those who fall short of what is expected during this critical period. Recalling the view of crisis as a "dangerous opportunity," the ways in which leaders exercise post-crisis leadership can establish a precedent for how the organization and its leaders respond to future exigencies; minimize the fear and distress experienced by many during the crisis; and serve as a catalyst for learning, healing, and growth in the period to follow the crisis.

A Values-Based Model for Post-Crisis Leadership

Many entities claim to be values-based organizations. These values help to anchor an institution around a set of shared principles that, when enacted, provide guidance and stability in pursuit of a mission.

Within higher education, for example, the realization of the tripartite mission of teaching, research, and service—and in some cases, community engagement and/or clinical excellence—hinges on the articulation, identification, and manifestation of some set of shared values. Many of the espoused values shared across colleges and universities include high morals and ethics, innovation and creativity, community engagement, sound governance, reflective practice, and a commitment to collaboration and team dynamics (Sutin & Jacob, 2016), in addition to public health and safety, accountability, diversity, equity and inclusion, academic freedom, social responsibility, and stewardship of public and donor resources. If we turn our attention to health-care organizations, the International Charter for Human Values in Healthcare highlights the human dimensions of health care that are fundamental to compassionate, ethical, and safe care and a host of core values and subvalues considered necessary for every health-care interaction (Rider et al., 2014). The five primary core values include compassion, respect for persons, commitment to integrity and ethical practice, commitment to excellence, and justice in health care.

During times of stability and normalcy, the embodiment and enactment of core values may come quite naturally to the members of an organization, often with little reflection or deliberation. However, drawing again upon Seeger and Ulmer's (2001) description, crises "are high impact events that often strip an organization to its core values" (p. 374); and amid the perilous conditions often present during periods of exigency, these values have the potential to recede from view as those with formal crisis responsibilities address the urgent demands of the moment (Gigliotti, 2022b). Crises, by their very nature, cause disruption and thereby have the potential to threaten an organization's core mission, purpose, or reason for existence. Organizational values are tested by crises, particularly those threatening the reputation and core competencies of the institution, yet these same values provide a compass for navigating terrain that for many may be foreign, frightening, or foggy. Leadership matters, and perhaps it matters most during times of turmoil. Given this need for values-based leadership, I will next explore what this might look like within the context of crisis and will conclude this introduction with a guiding framework for post-crisis leadership that will be deconstructed in the remaining chapters of this book.

The Work of Crisis Leadership

Crisis remains a ubiquitous condition for organizations of all kinds. Some crises are bound to specific institutions while others are far-reaching in scope, and, in many ways, organizational structure, traditions, and decision-making patterns might leave institutions vulnerable in responding to the complexity, urgency, and interdependent pressures that are characteristic of contemporary crises. At the same time, as described previously, the process of defining, labeling, and responding to organizational crises is a subjective, fluid, and improvisational endeavor that varies across individuals and is shaped by past crisis-like episodes, current responsibilities and expectations, and the degree of impact of the crisis. It is incumbent on formal and informal leaders to monitor potential issues that might develop into crises of significance; solicit input from stakeholders who may exhibit competing perceptions of what constitutes an organizational crisis; and engage in practices that reinforce, reflect, and reveal one's individual values and those held in regard by the organization during times of perceived crisis (Estes, 1983; Gigliotti, 2020a; Grint, 2005; Spector, 2019). An abundance of primary stakeholders can also complicate the work of crisis leadership, particularly when these individuals hold different and at times competing perceptions of crisis. From a social constructivist vantage point, crisis often lies in the eye of the beholder (Gigliotti, 2020a).

Although crises threaten the reputation of the organization and those individuals engaged in its leadership, a solely reputation-driven response to crises may be viewed as both constraining and short-sighted. Acting in accord with core values could enhance one's reputation, yet these values have the potential to be undermined or downplayed when responding to crises in ways that focus exclusively on preserving one's reputation. In some cases, leaders and institutions may feel pressured to act in ways that are incongruent with these espoused values due to the time pressures imposed by the crisis or under conditions of stress and stress-induced "tunnel vision" (Gigliotti, 2022b). For some, a restricted focus on preserving reputation can lead to acts of egregious behavior, such as active attempts to conceal the truth. Any attempt to de-emphasize sincere concern for those most affected by crises may limit dialogue, stifle learning, and stall the renewal and healing necessary during times of crisis (Gigliotti, 2019).

When faced with an organizational crisis, there are several models one might turn to for guidance. One especially relevant model is the crisis navigation framework (CNF; Stern, 2009), which draws upon interdisciplinary perspectives of crisis management and aligns with the values-based perspective emphasized throughout this book. The CNF consists of two parts, including a diagnostic tool for exploring key questions related to a crisis and six dimensions for leaders to consult when preparing for and coping with crises. Much of the crisis literature refers to the challenges of wading through environments and situations that are engulfed by "fog" and a high degree of uncertainty. Writing specifically about the uncertainty surrounding the COVID-19 pandemic, for example, Stephens et al. (2020) argue that "the only way for many of us, and for our communities and organizations, to sense the contours of this crisis is to walk straight into the fog and discover whatever is/was there" (p. 427). Both elements of the framework aim to improve sense making, decision making, and meaning-making during crises (Boin et al., 2017)—which involves a recognition of the contours of the situation and a multidimensional view of how best to proceed. In the first part of the CNF, Stern (2009) highlights three diagnostic questions for leadership consideration: "(1) What core values are at stake in this situation? (2) What are the key uncertainties associated with the situation and how can we reduce them? (3) How much time do we have or can we 'buy' ourselves?" (p. 191). The second part of the CNF consists of the following six dimensions: back (understanding the history); forward (looking ahead to the future); vertical (cooperation, coordination, and an effective division of labor within the organization); horizontal (cooperation, coordination, and an effective division of labor across organizations); in (managing the information flow into strategic decision-making groups); and out (optimizing information flows out of the top team) (Stern, 2009, pp. 191–199). As Stern writes, "A substantial body of theoretical and empirical studies strongly suggest that rigorous situational diagnosis and attention to the elements (temporal awareness, organizational complexity, and information flow) . . . can improve the likelihood of a successful crisis experience" (p. 199).

Distinct from crisis management, the emphasis on crisis leadership allows us to move from a mechanistic or tactical view of a leader's role in crisis to one that is arguably more systematic, proactive, and expansive (Gigliotti, 2019). Effective crisis leadership goes beyond delivering the most appropriate response(s) to the most appropriate audience(s) with the hope that these message(s) are interpreted as intended by the sender(s). This simplistic view of communication violates much of what is currently understood about human communication (Ruben & Gigliotti, 2016, 2017); instead, an understanding of communication might lead one to recognize the importance of understanding the organization's history with crisis, appreciating the diverse needs of one's stakeholders, and leading with integrity throughout the entire crisis process (i.e., before, during, and after the critical incident). Crisis leadership involves prevention and management, consistency and clarity, trust and transparency—with communication playing a critical role throughout each phase of any given crisis (Gigliotti, 2019). As DuBrin (2013) notes, crisis leaders demonstrate charisma, strategic thinking, and an ability to inspire and to express sadness and compassion. By forming and maintaining a reservoir of goodwill at the individual and collective levels, a foundation is built for authentic, values-centered dialogue when crises strike.

It seems likely that a values-driven reputation and history that serve an individual leader and collective organization well during times of normalcy are essential for effective leadership and performance during times of crisis, ultimately by providing a solid foundation upon which to stand when the ground below seems to be crumbling. Furthermore, by ensuring a clear articulation and deconstruction of core institutional values prior to a crisis, organizational leaders can help to cultivate a shared understanding regarding what these values represent and how they will be used to inform the decisions made during future crisis events. Leadership behaviors directly and indirectly model what is both expected and accepted in organizational life.

Crisis prevention, management, and communication are not unimportant. Rather, these components arguably are embedded in what is described in this book as "crisis leadership." It is increasingly important that leaders learn what is expected of them with regard to crisis prevention and management while also taking account of the centrality of communication in their leadership behaviors throughout *all* phases of a given crisis—pre-crisis, crisis, and post-crisis (Coombs, 2022). As Sellnow and Seeger (2020) remind us: "These events shatter the fundamental sense of normalcy, stability, and predictability we all count on in living our daily lives. They are disruptive, confusing, shocking, and intense events, and making sense of them and reestablishing some new normal requires communication" (p. 17).

Booker (2014) posits various leadership competencies that are most essential for each phase of the crisis process. These competencies include the detection of early warning signs in the environment; the strategic use of communication in preventing, preparing for, and containing the crisis; and the promotion of learning throughout the process and at the conclusion of the crisis (p. 19). As a more proactive and holistic approach to dealing with crises, crisis leadership's broader focus allows us to consider the range of behaviors required throughout all phases of crisis, including the need for risk-assessment tactics that precede a crisis to the learning processes that are rendered meaningful in their aftermath, all with an eye toward those crises that might be lurking on the horizon (Mitroff, 2004).

In summary, the act of crisis leadership requires a careful understanding of the types of risks that a unit, department, or institution is currently facing or might one day face, as well as a continual emphasis on learning throughout all phases of the crisis process (Gigliotti & Fortunato, 2021). Stretching beyond the preservation of one's reputation, the exigencies of crisis allow organizations and their leaders to demonstrate values-based leadership in ways that privilege dialogue with others and an ethic of care and concern for those most likely impacted by the crisis.

Referring to some of the early assumptions introduced at the outset of this book, crisis leadership—which takes account of leading before, during, and after crisis—is an imperative for leaders at all levels. Post-crisis leadership is a core dimension of crisis leadership; however, the complexities of leading in and through a crisis can contribute to the absence of attention directed to post-crisis leadership. The fatigue, frustration, and even trauma present in times of crisis have the potential to stall the healing and recovery that could result in the crisis aftermath. Often relegated as an afterthought in scholarship and practice, the ability to navigate the post-crisis period may in fact distinguish highly effective leaders and organizations.

Guiding Framework

With an underlying commitment to values-based, principle-oriented, and people-centered leadership practices, five practices seem to be particularly critical for leadership in the aftermath of crisis. These components arguably extend across organizational types, and despite the uniqueness of each crisis and the varying impact of different crisis types, the pain, fear, and uncertainty triggered by these crucible moments reinforce the need for leaders to embody each of the following practices to some degree. The five leadership practices, illustrated in figure 1, include a commitment to (a) encourage learning, (b) inspire growth, (c) stimulate meaning-making, (d) pursue reinvention, and (e) advance renewal. Each of

Post-crisis leadership framework				
Encourage learning	Inspire growth	Stimulate meaning-making	Pursue reinvention	Advance renewal

FIG. 1. Post-crisis leadership practices (author).

these practices relies on communication, and, as will be highlighted in the chapters to follow, these dimensions often result from the interplay of leaders, followers, and the unique contexts in which they are embedded.

Crises shatter, disrupt, and derail; they also create windows of opportunity for change, innovation, and the emergence of new ways of being. Furthermore, these events serve as crucible moments for individuals engaged in leadership. They are often high-stakes moments where attention is hyper-focused on the behaviors, actions, and decisions of those with formal decision-making authority. Situated within an environment ripe for potential crisis, the steps leaders choose to take to respond to crises establish a precedent for future emergency situations, and their responses are also deeply influenced by past experiences in crisis. The stakes are often higher for organizations that claim to be values-based, and one may hope these organizations will serve as standard-bearers in responding with agility, grace, and a deeply rooted commitment to the enduring principles upon which these institutions stand. The model outlined in this book is intended to serve as a useful guide for scholars and practitioners seeking to better understand and engage in values-based post-crisis leadership.

1

Encourage Learning

Crises have the potential to stimulate individual and organizational learning, and, as discussed in this chapter, the ability to encourage learning is a key component of effective leadership in the aftermath of crisis. This post-crisis period may provide appropriate conditions from which to analyze the pertinent factors, reflect on major lessons derived from the crisis, and explore strengths and areas for improvement regarding the decisions and actions made in response to the crisis. These learning practices can center on an individual experience or the experiences of a specific unit, department, or institution. Careful and critical learning in groups, teams, and organizations is possible in the aftermath of crisis; however, the ability to engage in the process of collective learning often relies on a dedicated and deliberate approach to leadership. This is particularly true if the desired goal of such learning activities is to inform organizational policies, practices, or procedures.

This period in the life cycle of a crisis can be used to peel back the layers of the incident and critically explore the dynamics that might have contributed to the event's emergence. Through the adoption of formal tools, such as an incident postmortem or after-action review, or through the use of informal methods to stimulate individual and group reflection in the aftermath of crisis, an intentional attempt to encourage learning can lead to appropriate corrective action and a thorough examination of the underlying factors that might inhibit organizational effectiveness. By adopting and routinizing such learning processes and structures, leaders at all levels can enhance the learning capabilities of their unit, department, or organization and ultimately contribute to a climate in which post-incident learning becomes a standard practice. This chapter will synthesize relevant concepts from the literature on organizational learning, explore the extent to which colleges and universities may be viewed as learning organizations, and advance several implications for the work of post-crisis leadership. Examples from public after-action reports related to the Texas A&M bonfire collapse and the Virginia Tech mass shooting will be integrated throughout this chapter to provide insight into the layers of learning that might be possible in the aftermath of crisis and to draw attention to strategies for encouraging learning in the aftermath of disruption.

Learning in Times of Crisis

Advancements in information and communication technologies, the expansion of globalization and increased global connectedness, and the pace of exponential change make the subject of organizational learning one of ongoing scholarly and applied interest. As Argyris (1977) notes, "Organizational learning is a process of detecting and correcting error. Error is for our purposes any feature of knowledge or knowing that inhibits learning" (p. 116). In their seminal work on theory in practice, Argyris and Schön (1974) claim that people have mental maps that serve as guides for how to act in situations, and these maps often come into conflict with previously espoused theories. Argyris (1980) suggests that effectiveness results from developing congruence between theory-in-use and espoused theory. The discrepancy between the ideal and the real—or between the ways in which we think we might behave and our actual behaviors—makes essential the practice of reflection. Schön (1987) describes reflection as "a dialogue of thinking and doing through which I become more skillful" (p. 31), and this habit of reflective practice leads to greater self-awareness, the development and acquisition of new knowledge, and a broader understanding of the issues we might be confronted with (Osterman, 1990). Schön (1987) differentiates three types of reflection:

- *Reflection-on-action*—looking back on personal and group experiences to evaluate reasoning processes used.
- *Reflection-in-action*—occurs as we watch ourselves in action.
- *Reflection-for-action*—refers to the predictive process for forecasting how we will use what we have learned based on the previous two forms of reflection.

Kolb's (1984) writing on experiential learning, rooted in the tradition of learning theory (Dewey, 1974; Piaget, 1936; Vygotsky, 1978), reinforces this view of learning that is dependent on the integration of experience and reflection. Put differently, learning only becomes possible through the act of reflection, and, as Kolb (1984) acknowledges, learning requires the acquisition of abstract concepts that can then be applied flexibly in a wide range of situations, experiences, and encounters.

Within the context of organizational learning, it is important to distinguish between what Argyris and Schön (1978) describe as *single-loop learning* and *double-loop learning*. In single-loop learning, people, organizations, or groups modify their actions according to the difference between expected and actual outcomes. Single-loop learning occurs "whenever an error is detected and corrected without questioning or altering the underlying values of the system" (Argyris, 1999, p. 68). Thus, when things go wrong or when individuals encounter unpleasant or unintended outcomes, single-loop learning allows for corrective action or the pursuit of an alternative strategy. Double-loop learning, on the other hand, occurs when "mismatches are corrected by first examining and altering the governing variables and then the actions" (p. 68). Such learning may lead to an alteration in the underlying variables; a shift in the way in which strategies and consequences are framed; and perhaps even a modification of an organization's underlying norms, policies, and objectives.

As we explore these concepts within the context of crisis, reflective practice, experiential learning, and single-loop and double-loop learning take on heightened significance for leaders during times of disruption, although the competing expectations of the moment may not allow adequate time for the enactment of such practices. Crises heighten the pressure for urgent action and decision making, create uncertainty regarding the issue at hand and the root cause(s) that may have contributed to it, and intensify the emotions surrounding the event or series of events. When responding to a crisis, it is often necessary to address both what is happening and what might need to happen to prevent the situation from happening again in the future, and in the spirit of double-loop learning, we might also examine the underlying assumptions and conditions that made such an outcome possible. Acknowledging the value of increasing organizational capacity for double-loop learning, such an approach is necessary for making informed decisions in rapidly changing and often uncertain contexts (Argyris 1982, 1990). Double-loop learning demands self-awareness, honesty or candor, and the willingness to take responsibility (Argyris 1982, 1990); and the conditions of crisis and demands of the moment may stand in the way of such efforts. As Antonacopoulou and Sheaffer (2014) write, "When faced with crisis, managers and their organizations may be paralyzed not only owing to coping difficulties but because they face a knowledge and learning crisis. Such a crisis presents uncertainties about the engagement with the unknown, especially when existing knowledge and learning are proving insufficient to address these complexities" (p. 9). In short, the conditions of crisis both necessitate and complicate learning.

Echoing the themes of reflective practice and single-loop and double-loop learning, Antonacopoulou and Sheaffer (2014) conceptualize *learning in crisis* as a "mode of learning that is in tune with the emerging conditions that contribute to creating what culminates into and is perceived to be a crisis" (p. 6). Their perspective highlights the act of learning as ongoing, practical, and reliant upon balancing both the *emergence* and *emergency* (p. 8). This focus on the practice of learning in the context of crisis management or crisis leadership is the subject of an increasing body of research, and, as suggested in this chapter, it is a critical imperative for leaders attempting to navigate the period following the crisis. Given that crises of significant magnitude are increasing in frequency and intensity (Helsloot et al., 2012; James et al., 2011; Perrow, 1984; Seeger, 2018), the rate at which organizations learn may become the determining factor in their ability to adapt or survive (Schwandt & Marquadt, 2000).

Institutions of Higher Education as Learning Organizations

The lessons gleaned from one's own experience and the experiences of others can be interpreted, maintained, accumulated, and acted upon within the routines, traditions, and habits of an organization (Fiol & Lyles, 1985; Huber, 1991; Levitt & March, 1988). Some organizations may be characterized as *learning organizations*, which, to borrow from Garvin's (1993) definition, represents organizations that are "skilled at creating, acquiring, and transferring knowledge, and at modifying [their] behavior to reflect new knowledge and insights." This definition echoes the work of Senge (2006), who defines a learning organization as one where "people continually expand their capacity to create the results they truly desire, where new and expansive patterns of thinking are nurtured, where collective aspiration is set free, and where people are continually learning to see the whole together" (p. 3). These definitions signal the presence of both single-loop and double-loop learning and the cultivation of an environment where individuals feel safe to stretch their thinking, challenge conventional wisdom, and adopt a systems perspective in better understanding the relationship among the various parts of the organization.

Systems thinking is an analytical approach to understanding and responding to the dynamics of complex systems in order to enable learning, adaptation, and more effective functioning in pursuit of shared goals (Senge, 2006). A systems thinking approach shifts our perspective from the *organization* as a static structure to a more intentional focus on *organizing* as an ongoing, dynamic, and fluid process (Gigliotti & Goldthwaite, 2021). This shift in orientation requires us to devote greater attention to the interdependencies present in organizational life and to engage in a continuous and systematic scan of the environment to better forecast trends, learn from other parts of the ecosystem, and adapt to change. The often chaotic and unpredictable environment within which modern organizations are embedded requires them to become learning organizations, where activities such as "systematic problem solving, experimentation with new approaches, learning from their own experiences and past history, learning from the experiences and best practices of others, and transferring knowledge quickly and efficiently throughout the organization" are widely practiced (Garvin, 1993, p. 81). Systems thinking is one of five "component technologies" or "disciplines" associated with the creation and cultivation of a learning organization, in addition to these other variables:

- *Personal mastery*—clarification of one's vision, development of a tolerance for change and ambiguity, and engagement in the unbiased examination of events and circumstances.
- *Mental models*—examination of one's assumptions about how the world works or should work to better understand how behaviors are shaped.
- *Shared vision*—development of shared purposes, values, goals, mission, and vision.
- *Team learning*—thinking together through dialogue and discussion to advance shared understanding and a collective commitment to action. (p. 3)

These practices highlight the importance of cultivating relationships both within and beyond the boundaries of a given organization and engaging in a multilevel analysis of the system and the broader context within which a system operates. A commitment to such practices can help the organization become "more skilled at creating, acquiring, and transferring knowledge, and at modifying its behavior to reflect new knowledge and insights" (Garvin, 1993, p. 3). The ability to engage in these organizational practices is helpful during times of stability and becomes especially critical in supporting the organization during times of perceived disruption or crisis.

Learning manifests itself differently across organizations. Örtenblad and Koris (2014, p. 175) provide a useful typology of the four types of learning organizations:

- *Learning at work*—an organization in which the employees learn while working (as opposed to learning at formal courses).
- *Organizational learning*—an organization with an awareness of the need for different levels of learning and the storing of knowledge in the organizational memory (rather than in the individuals)
- *Climate for learning*—an organization that facilitates the learning of its individuals by creating a positive atmosphere that makes learning easy and natural, offers space and time for experimenting and reflection, and tolerates failure.
- *Learning structure*—an organization with a flexible, decentralized, informal, and organic team-based structure that enables its members to make their own decisions in order to quickly satisfy continuously changing customer expectations, and that needs continual learning and redundancy to occur in order for it to attain and retain flexibility.

Leaders play an important role in helping to build and sustain a learning organization. As Renesch and Chawla (2006) note, "In essence, the leaders are those building the new organization and its capabilities. They are the ones 'walking ahead,' regardless of their management position or hierarchical authority" (p. 34).

Based on the above definitions and criteria, it is easy to take the position of viewing institutions of higher education as learning organizations. As Nannerl Keohane (2006), former president of Wellesley College and Duke University, describes the "moral purpose" of the academy: "Colleges and universities play a crucial part in determining whether humanity will indeed have a future, and what it will be like. Our institutions have significant moral purposes; we are not just collections of loosely affiliated persons with convergent or conflicting interests, but institutions that make a difference in the world through pursuing our basic goals" (p. 2). Given their commitment to truth, inquiry, and lifelong learning in pursuit of this moral purpose—and an enduring commitment to the mission of teaching, research, service, and, in some cases, community engagement and/or clinical excellence—colleges and universities would seem to be model learning organization archetypes. Although institutions of higher education are designed to promote learning, and although they may seem to be ideal incubators for practices that are consistent with the learning organization literature, some advise caution in labeling all colleges and universities as learning organizations (Bak, 2012; Miller, 2020; Örtenblad & Koris, 2014; Reese, 2017). White and Weathersby (2005) detail several of the obstacles that may prevent colleges and universities from becoming learning organizations, including conundrums of strategy, structure, and culture, as well as academic culture clashes. Complacency, fear, siloes, and the resistance to change may also stand in the way of organizational learning, in addition to the presence of paralysis, trauma, and instability that may result from organizational crises.

Learning organizations require structures for accountability, fluid communication within and across units, and a climate that both encourages and celebrates the creation, acquisition, transfer, and application of knowledge. With a goal of adopting some practices that are consistent with a learning organization, Örtenblad and Koris (2014) advise colleges and universities "to increase their double-loop learning, increase their efforts in providing a learning climate as well as interdisciplinary cooperation, and listen more to their staff and other stakeholders . . . while avoiding becoming [overly] organic in the sense of being student-customer oriented, flexible, and informal" (p. 205). The ability to become a learning organization may serve as a competitive advantage for some institutions of higher education (Bui & Baruch, 2010a, 2010b, 2012), and this becomes especially important in preparing for, responding to, and recovering from institutional and environmental crises.

Encouraging Learning in the Aftermath of Crisis

Organizational learning is an important component of one's response to a crisis (Pearson & Clair, 1998). Organizations that learn may limit their exposure to similar problems in the future (Argyris, 1977; Carmeli & Schaubroeck, 2008; James et al., 2011; Wooten & James, 2004), and a learning mindset may very well differentiate the crisis-prepared organization from the crisis-prone organization (Weick & Sutcliffe, 2001). Learning during times of crisis can occur within institutions, across organizations within an industry (Nathan & Kovoor-Misra, 2002), and across sectors (Crichton et al., 2009). Facilitators of organizational learning during crisis include formal systems and practices; objectives, priorities, and resources; organizational culture and climate; and individual attitudes (Pauchant & Mitroff, 1992), whereas the impediments include psychological and cultural barriers (Argyris, 1990; Pauchant & Mitroff, 1992) and organizational structures and leadership barriers (Dierkes et al., 2001). Both sets of barriers are reflected in Moynihan's (2008) list of potential barriers to effective learning during crises:

- The high consequentiality of crises makes trial and error learning prohibitive.
- Crises require interorganizational rather than organizational learning.
- There is a lack of relevant experience, heuristics, SOPs (standard operating procedures), or technologies to draw on.

- The scope of learning required is greater than for routine situations.
- The ambiguity of previous experience gives rise to faulty lesson drawing.
- Crises narrow focus and limit information processing.
- There is a rigidity of response: actors recycle old solutions to new problems.
- Political dynamics give rise to bargaining and suboptimal decisions.
- Crises provoke defensive postures and denial of the problem, responsibility, or error.
- Crises provoke opportunism as actors focus on their positive role. (p. 351)

In much the same way one might assume that all colleges and universities are learning organizations, there is also a tendency to take learning for granted in the aftermath of crisis. In his seminal work on disasters, for example, Turner (1976) writes that "when the immediate effects [of a disaster] subsided, it becomes possible to move toward something like a full cultural readjustment . . . of beliefs, norms, and precautions, making them compatible with the newly gained understanding of the world" (p. 382). However, as a growing body of research suggests, organizations and their leaders may express some resistance to learning from crisis (Brockner & James, 2008; Elliott, 2009; Pauchant & Mitroff, 1992; D. Smith & Elliott, 2007; Toft & Reynolds, 1997). Furthermore, as D. Smith and Elliott (2007) note, the barriers to learning can themselves generate the conditions that allow an incident to escalate into a crisis—making what Turner (1976) refers to as full cultural adjustment an ideal that is rarely achieved (p. 520). In further exploring these barriers to effective learning from crisis events, D. Smith and Elliott (2007) draw attention to three key, yet distinct, relationships: (1) *learning for crisis* (the process of developing reactive capabilities for how best to respond to crisis events), (2) *learning as crisis* (whereby focusing upon one set of threats create a new set of unforeseen hazards and difficulties, triggering what might be described as a secondary crisis), and (3) *learning from crisis* (the process of learning from one's own experiences and from the experiences of others).

By way of example, we can now turn our attention to two historic university crises—the Texas A&M bonfire collapse and the Virginia Tech mass shooting—and the type of learning documented in their commissioned reports (Gigliotti, 2022b).

For ninety years, students at Texas A&M built a bonfire on campus each autumn. According to the university's website, "the Fightin' Texas Aggie Bonfire symbolized every Aggie's 'burning desire' to beat the University of Texas in football. Attracting between 30,000 and 70,000 people each year to watch it burn, Bonfire became a symbol of the deep and unique camaraderie that is the Aggie Spirit" (Texas A&M University, n.d.). On November 18, 1999, at 2:42 A.M., the fifty-nine-foot bonfire collapsed during construction, sending more than a million pounds of timber crashing to the ground, killing eleven students and one former student and injuring twenty-seven others (Morse, 1999; Ramirez, 2019). A special commission formed in the aftermath of the incident attributed the collapse to both physical and organizational factors (U.S. Fire Administration, 1999). The physical factor included a containment failure in the bottom layer of logs. The organizational failure, according to the report, involved "the absence of an appropriate written design or design process, a cultural bias impeding risk identification, and the lack of a proactive risk management approach" (p. 3).

In addition to these variables, a failure in learning also may have contributed to the crisis. Five years prior to the tragedy at Texas A&M, in 1994, more than eighteen inches of rain fell on the Bryan-College Station area the week before the bonfire. According to LeBas (1999), "The ground underneath the stack of logs shifted, causing the base of the structure to buckle. Bonfire leaders decided to topple the nearly-finished stack and start building again." The decision to lay two tons of lime hardened the ground for subsequent fires, but a failure to learn from this collapse resulted in missed opportunities to identify structural problems for future bonfires. As documented in the commission's report into the 1999 disaster, "A number of people claim that [the 1994 mishap] should have been interpreted as a warning sign. Yet, it was attributed by everyone involved to wet and unstable ground, not structural integrity. In fact, structural integrity was praised because it required heavy equipment to pull the stack apart. It is easy to see why nothing triggered a design re-examination. It is also easy to see why Bonfire friends and foes alike agree—the 1999 collapse came as a complete surprise" (U.S. Fire Administration, 1999, p. 29). As the report goes on to note, "The evidence of ongoing problems with Bonfire is so overwhelming that collectively these problems should have triggered a broader overall re-examination of Bonfire—one that included Bonfire design and construction. Unfortunately, this did not occur" (p. 31).

Following the crisis, Texas A&M University president Ray Bowen suspended the bonfire for several years and integrated lessons learned from the commissioned report into the revived tradition in 2002. Some of these changes included a more stable single-tier "teepee" design using logs delivered to campus; oversight, supervision, and inspection by professional engineers; the elimination of all-night building shifts; and a crackdown on alcohol consumption at the bonfire site (Ramirez, 2019). Student Bonfire, a nonprofit organization no longer directly affiliated with the university, continues to hold a modified annual bonfire before the last home football game.

Missed and overlooked clues were also part of the storyline in a major crisis to impact the Blacksburg, Virginia, campus of Virginia Polytechnic Institute and State University (Virginia Tech) on the morning of April 16, 2007. In less than three hours, Seung-Hui Cho put an end to thirty-three lives, including his own, resulting in what is now recognized as the third-deadliest mass shooting in U.S. history. Following this act of "domestic terrorism," people from across the world came together to embrace the

Virginia Tech community (Armstrong & Frykberg, 2007). At 12:41 P.M. the same day, the administration delivered the first public statement regarding the shooting. As university president Charles W. Steger expressed, "The university is shocked and indeed horrified that this would befall us" (Harris, 2007). As he would eventually go on to acknowledge in his nationally televised convocation remarks: "It is overwhelming, almost paralyzing, yet our hearts and our minds call us to come together, to share our individual attempts to comprehend the incomprehensible, to make sense of the senseless, and to find ways for our community to heal. And, slowly and painfully but inevitably, to begin to heal and to again move forward. We are very grateful that we do not have to travel this path alone" (Steger, 2007).

The commissioned report that followed this tragedy points to a variety of missed cues and a collapse in organizational communication. Some of the major shortfalls included a failure to share relevant information regarding the eventual shooter due to widespread misinterpretation of privacy laws and the loss of records in the transition from Cho's high school and college, a premature conclusion by public safety officials in what was initially perceived to be an isolated domestic violence incident, and a delayed alert to the university community of up to two hours (Virginia Tech Review Panel, 2007).

The Virginia Tech shooting led to national policy changes and a review of institutional protocols for risk prevention, emergency communication, and crisis plans for active shooter situations. As noted by Gene Deisinger, who consulted with Virginia Tech officials after the shooting and who later accepted a position as the university's deputy chief of police and director of threat management services, the mass shooting "highlighted the whole spectrum of emergency preparedness and management in higher education, from prevention and mitigation to response capabilities" (Winn, 2017). As he noted, "It wasn't just the university, a lot of local agencies were overwhelmed as well. It showed that campus emergency preparedness couldn't develop by itself. It has to develop in concert with community resources and capabilities" (Winn, 2017). The shooting eventually led to an amendment of the Clery Act, the federal law that requires institutions of higher education not only to collect and report campus crime statistics, but also to develop a multimodal emergency warning system to dispatch information as quickly as possible.

A retrospective review of the bonfire tragedy at Texas A&M and the active shooter event at Virginia Tech highlights flaws in information processing, communication, and learning that occurred both prior to and during these incidents. Additionally, informed by the lessons learned, these incidents have contributed to changes in crisis and risk prevention and management efforts across higher education. History has a way of repeating itself, and the ability to learn from the past can prove valuable when responding to the contemporary crises of our time. Although the dynamics may be different, we see echoes of the Texas A&M and Virginia Tech crises in some of the more recent tragedies to transpire across higher education, including the countless active shooter situations, hazing-related deaths, and structural building and pedestrian bridge collapses that resulted in the loss of life. A more proactive and systematic approach to learning in the aftermath of crisis may help to prevent the occurrence of future tragedies. In these cases, learning becomes more than an intellectual exercise—it is a practice with life-or-death implications—and we must not forget the direct and indirect impact of leadership on individual, group, and organizational learning activities (Lundqvist et al., 2023).

In both of the above cases we find examples of the three types of crisis learning (D. Smith & Elliott, 2007). With the intention of *learning for crisis*, prior planning allowed the institutions to prepare for the bonfire event and active shooter situation; however, the experiences associated with both crises and the lessons gleaned from these unfortunate events contributed to how Texas A&M, Virginia Tech, and colleges and universities could learn from the crises. And in what D. Smith and Elliott describe as *learning as crisis*, both critical incidents illustrate individual and collective learning practices that perhaps challenged the deeply held assumptions and beliefs among key stakeholders. As the authors describe this type of learning, "Although the motivation to learn may arise 'artificially' during the pre-crisis stage, it appears more likely that a challenge to core beliefs will arise from the direct experiences of decision makers during the other two stages. In one sense, learning as crisis may be seen as a driver of 'learning for and from crisis'" (p. 525).

As we fast forward to consider critical incidents facing contemporary leaders within higher education, the challenges of the day demand a learning orientation. For example, at the time of writing, university presidents and chancellors are under significant pressure to respond to evolving global conflict in the Middle East and the rippling effect of these incidents throughout our institutions. The complexities of the moment demand care, sensitivity, and humanity—and they also require a willingness to learn from members of the community, members of one's leadership team, and others across the higher education landscape who are navigating similar tensions. The desire to learn, the ability to engage in dialogue, and the humility to acknowledge the inherent tensions and inadequacies that accompany public responses to such contentious matters will likely continue to serve as a guide for how colleges and universities navigate issues related to global conflict, academic freedom, and free speech. And certainly, as we long for stability and peace on the international stage, the ability to cultivate opportunities for listening and learning during the aftermath of these crises will remain critical.

Considerations for Post-Crisis Leadership Action

As the dust settles in the period following a crisis, leaders may use the opportunity to take stock of recent events and devote time to engage in meaningful reflection and dialogue with representatives from their unit, department, or organization. In the spirit of exercising learning through meaningful listening, James and Wooten

(2022a) encourage a consideration of the following questions in order to leverage the perspective of others:

- Do you currently have access to diverse voices and sources of information within your team or organization, or even beyond its boundaries?
- Do you routinely build other team members' ideas or feedback into your decision making?
- What systems or processes might you need to put into place to surface and capture multi-stakeholder perspectives? (pp. 5–6)

In addition to considering these process-oriented questions for soliciting stakeholder input, a common strategy in the aftermath of crisis is to assign a committee or task force to conduct a formal incident postmortem or after-action review. This post-incident review convenes individuals to discuss the details of an incident: why it happened, what impact it had on different parts of the organization, what actions were taken to mitigate it and resolve it, and what should be done to prevent it from happening again. Ideally, a structured approach to these conversations can reveal key learning insights in preparation for the next crisis and can help to build trust among members of the team.

One approach to conducting this formal review involves *process tracing*, which George and Bennett (2005) define as a "method [that] attempts to identify the intervening causal process—the causal chain and causal mechanism—between an independent variable (or variables) and the outcome of the dependent variable" (p. 206). As a social science methodology, process tracing typically involves three stages: theorization about causal mechanisms linking causes and outcomes, analysis of the observable empirical manifestations of theorized mechanisms, and the complementary use of comparative methods to enable generalizations of findings from single case studies to other causally similar cases (Beach, 2017). As it relates to the focus of crisis analysis, Stern et al. (2014) offer an integrative method for case reconstruction and dissection which can contribute to a more systematic and multidimensional understanding of crisis issues. In their published postmortem analysis of the London bombings of July 2005, the authors use an adapted version of the process tracing method focusing on case reconstruction and decision-making occasion analysis. The method consists of four steps:

1. *Contextualization*—put the crisis into its proper historical, institutional/organizational, and political context.
2. *Chronology/narrative*—reconstruct the course of events in a chronological manner using available empirical material.
3. *Decision occasions*—break down the crisis into occasions for decision making based on the responses to various stimuli during the event and examine problem framing, decision making, and implementation; and to identify the result of a given decision occasion.
4. *Thematic comparison*—engage in a comparative analysis of themes to emerge from former research and those that emerge from the review of the selected crisis. (p. 3)

They go on to detail the following questions for consideration during each of these steps:

1. *Contextualization*: Does the crisis center on a novel and relatively unexpected issue or is there a previous history of and legacy from previous similar (or other paradigm shifting) contingencies? What are the key features of the pre-crisis institutional/ organizational/political environments?
2. *Chronology/narrative*: What triggers the crisis and motivates key decision makers to act at various junctures?
3. *Decision occasions*: Which problems were regarded as the most important ones for the decision makers and what decisions and results were involved in the case?
4. *Thematic comparison*: In what ways does this crisis compare to previous crises and what exemplary (or inferior) practices might be considered in the future? (pp. 3–5)

Other common questions that might be used to structure an after-action review include the following:

- What was expected to happen?
- What occurred?
- What went well and why?
- What can be improved and how?

In addition to identifying areas for improvement, standard after-action review templates might include an identification of corrective actions, responsible parties, and target deadlines.

James and Wooten (2022b) present the following questions that might also prompt learning during a post-crisis review:

- Who will you assemble among your stakeholders to include in your post-crisis review, and what questions do you need to ask: How might you have done things differently to achieve different outcomes?
- How will you ensure that failure as well as success becomes a learning opportunity?
- How will you determine, document, and share the lessons and takeaways of this crisis, and what actions will you take to drive necessary change in your culture, systems, or processes? (p. 122)

In the spirit of encouraging learning in the aftermath of crisis, the following recommendations may serve as a guide:

- Ensure broad participation from diverse stakeholders on post-incident review committees.
- Provide formal and informal opportunities to analyze, debrief, and learn from the experiences of past crises.
- Solicit feedback from across the organization as part of the postmortem process and meaningfully integrate this input into the after-action review.

- Pose questions to stimulate both single-loop and double-loop learning in the aftermath of crisis.
- Design opportunities to learn from exemplary crisis leadership practices based on the experiences of others from across disciplines, institutions, and sectors.
- Encourage employees throughout the organization to create a learning organization mindset through a continual and systematic review of the organizational culture, established structures and policies, and leadership behaviors that might either encourage or hinder organizational learning.

Leaders who engage in effective post-crisis strategies to encourage learning can help to build capacity in preparing for the inevitable difficult moments that lie ahead. As a centerpiece of their framework, James and Wooten (2022) reinforce the importance of learning by indicating the following: "You cannot prepare for any future crisis without first *learning the lessons that experience has to teach*. Your capacity to prepare for what lies beyond the next crisis is only as good as your ability to learn from the lessons it shares" (p. 111). Post-crisis learning can help units, departments, and organizations withstand the pressures of future crises and bounce back with greater ease and effectiveness, as will be explored in chapter 2, on resilience.

2

Cultivate Resilience

Crises have a way of exposing the vulnerability of the human condition and disturbing the sense of normalcy and stability to which one might be accustomed. These periods of disruption for individuals, groups, organizations, and communities also tend to reveal the inadequacy of the systems and structures upon which we depend. Crises have the potential to lead to a reconsideration of common approaches and paradigms and to the questioning and challenging of previously accepted norms and assumptions. Situations involving the loss of life or those that threaten people's health and well-being in particular can lead to despair, vulnerability, and anguish. However, crises can also catalyze reinvention, renewal, and restoration, and, as discussed in this chapter, leaders play an important role in helping to cultivate resilience and inspire growth in the aftermath of tragedy. As the dust settles in the period following a crisis, leaders will need to draw upon the strength and determination of those most impacted by it and create opportunities for sustained growth in dealing with future adversity.

The topic of resilience is one of increased significance for those interested in the study and practice of leadership. As the headline of a December 29, 2022, *Harvard Business Review* piece questioned, "Was 2022 the Year of Resilience?" (Amico, 2022). In response to the converging crises of the 2020s, "resilience" remains a common buzzword in the scholarly and professional literature—and it is a topic worthy of attention for post-crisis leadership. In a write-up for the American Psychological Association's *Monitor on Psychology*, Abrams (2022) wrote about these converging crises in the United States—including the pandemic, economic challenges, political polarization, climate-related disasters, and mass shootings—and their effect on well-being, safety, and efficacy. Referring to what psychologist Roxane Cohen Silver calls a "cascade of collective traumas that the nation is facing together," Abrams (2022) documents heightened levels of stress across the country and a dulling sense of compassion in light of the overwhelming scale of these crises—what cognitive psychologists characterize as *psychic numbing*. During an age of unprecedented risk and the deadly arithmetic of compassion, the more people who die in an incident of mass violence, "the less we care" (Slovic & Västfjäll, 2015). Abrams (2022) quotes Rinad Beidas, a professor of psychiatry, medical ethics and health policy, and medicine, who suggests that "we're not starting at a place where everybody is healthy and thriving. Our reserves are depleted as a nation and our young people are suffering."

The ongoing sources of tension across the higher education landscape detailed in the introduction pose significant threats to colleges and universities and contribute to conditions that have been described as both unstable and unsustainable. The resilience of higher education remains a topic of timely importance, but what exactly does resilience mean? According to the *Oxford English Dictionary*, resilience is "the capacity to recover quickly from difficulties" (Oxford University Press, n.d.). Other common definitions of human resilience describe people's ability to bounce back or reintegrate after difficult experiences, with an emphasis on adaptation, adjustment, transformation, and fortitude. For example, the American Psychological Association's definition of resilience points to "the process of adapting well in the face of adversity, trauma, tragedy, threats, or significant sources of stress—such as family and relationship problems, serious health problems, or workplace and financial stressors." Or, as Sutcliffe and Vogus (2003) define it, resilience is "the maintenance of positive adjustments under challenging conditions" (p. 95). An individual's ability to withstand and recover from these difficult experiences has implications for those seeking to lead and influence others in a post-crisis context. These difficult experiences for individuals, groups, organizations, and communities can also create unique windows of opportunity for growth. In this chapter, we will take a closer look at some of the relevant streams of literature related to resilience and post-traumatic growth and explore various principles and points of connection for leaders seeking to cultivate resilience and inspire growth in the aftermath of crisis.

An Overview of Resilience

Traditional research on the study of resilience in psychology tends to focus on the resilience of individuals and the extent to which they are able to bounce back or reintegrate after experiencing some degree of loss, trauma, or difficulty. From a material science perspective, an image of resilience as "super material" centers on the ability of individuals or organizations to absorb strain and maintain their shape (Porac, 2002). Another way of viewing resilience is through a developmental lens—an approach that is common in the child and family development literature (Masten, 2014). As summarized by Sutcliffe and Vogus (2003), "Resilience from a developmental perspective does not merely emerge in response to specific interruptions or jolts, but rather develops over time from continually handling risks, stresses, and strains" (p. 96). Within the context of positive organizational scholarship, resilient responses to challenging conditions by individuals, groups, and organizations are "thought to add both to the strength of the current entity and also to the strength of the future entity, in that resilience is the continuing ability to use internal and external resources successfully to resolve issues" (p. 96).

In her communication theory of resilience (CTR), Buzzanell (2010) argues that resilience does not reside in the individual. As she writes, "Rather than an individual phenomenon that someone either possesses or does not, resilience is developed, sustained, and grown through discourse, interaction, and material considerations" (p. 1). Communicative theorizing on resilience focuses on the process of resilience—as a collaborative exchange that is constituted through communicative interactions for which people prepare, continuously learn to enact, and engage strategically (Buzzanell, 2010, 2018). The writing on CTR describes the ways in which individuals, groups, organizations, and communities engage in the active construction and co-construction of resilience (Houston & Buzzanell, 2020). As S. R. Wilson et al. (2021) note: "CTR asserts that resilience is both reactive and anticipatory. Although resilience is not conceptualized as a trait, CTR does recognize that some individuals—based on prior experiences and circumstances—may be better positioned than others to enact resilience (or that the same person may be better positioned at some points than others)" (p. 481). According to this theory, resilience is cultivated communicatively and often collectively through the enactment of five subprocesses: (1) crafting a new normalcy, (2) affirming or anchoring important identities during difficult times, (3) using and/or maintaining salient communication networks, (4) looking beyond conventional ways of thinking about and doing life by putting alternative logics to work, and (5) foregrounding productive action while backgrounding unproductive behaviors or negative feelings (Buzzanell, 2010, 2018; Buzzanell & Houston, 2018). See table 1 for a more detailed description of each of these resilience processes along with examples of each one.

Building out this communication-centered view of resilience further, Barbour et al. (2018) describe how the "organizations and interorganizational systems upon which we depend to keep us safe in a risky world rely on communication" (p. 154). As the authors go on to describe, "Communication choices made in day-to-day work have important implications during emergencies, and the

TABLE 1 Conceptual Definitions of the Five CTR Processes

RESILIENCE PROCESS	CONCEPTUAL DEFINITION	EXAMPLES OF THE PROCESS
Crafting normalcy	Talking/acting/interacting so as to help create a sense that things are "normal" (i.e., getting back to a sense of the prior normal and/or creating a new normal)	Maintaining, adapting and/or creating routines (e.g., schedules, media habits) Talking about how things are normal Focusing on mundane accomplishments that help create a sense of normal
Affirming identity anchors	Performing salient identities and values (e.g., answers to questions such as "who am I/who are we/who do I [we] aspire to be?) that may be challenged by, provide meaning during, and help guide responses to disruption	Affirming gendered family roles (e.g., father, breadwinner, military spouse) Following/strengthening spiritual beliefs Expressing affiliation with sports teams (e.g., dress, online activities) Calling upon cultural philosophies/values (e.g., family honor in China)
Maintaining and using comm. networks	Maintaining, growing, and drawing on strong and weak network ties (i.e., social capital) for needed resources and support	Reaching out to family, friends, acquaintances, peers, and professionals (face-to-face or online) Posting resumes online (job loss) Reaching out to governmental/non-profit organizations during times of disruption
Constructing alternative logics	Moving beyond conventional ways of thinking/acting and creating alternative (often paradoxical) ways of anticipating/reframing/responding to disruptions	Using humor to make light of difficult times Watching/performing standup comedy Using metaphors to reframe situations in unexpected or ironic ways (e.g., a patient calling a cancer diagnosis a "gift") Reinterpreting policies, creatively working around the system to get things done

(*continued*)

TABLE 1 (continued)

RESILIENCE PROCESS	CONCEPTUAL DEFINITION	EXAMPLES OF THE PROCESS
Foregrounding productive action while backgrounding negative feelings	Deliberately taking productive actions while backgrounding unproductive feelings/actions; acknowledging one has the right to feel anger/loss while recognizing these feelings can be counterproductive to more important goals	Choosing to rebuild one's life and feel proud of one's "difference" while acknowledging painful experiences (marginalized family members) Pursuing job options and creating positive online/interview image despite being angry about having been laid off (job loss)

SOURCE: S. R. Wilson et al. (2021).

logics underlying those choices may have powerful effects on the forms that reliability, resilience, and safety take" (p. 155). The patterns and practices of communication serve an important function for how resilience is made manifest in responding to and recovering from crises. The communicative enactment of resilience has the potential to play out during each phase of a crisis—in preparing for potential crises that might demand resilience (Doerfel & Prezelj, 2017), in responding to the trigger events that create a sense of loss and disrupt people's lives (Buzzanell, 2010, 2018), and in cultivating, recognizing, and restoring systems of resilience during the return to stability or normalcy.

In addition to the communicative theorizing on resilience, the expanding research on the topic of organizational resilience enriches how we might understand the leader's role in the aftermath of crisis. According to Vogus and Sutcliffe (2007), the concept of organizational resilience provides "insight into how organizations and the individuals and units of which they are comprised continue to achieve desirable outcomes amidst adversity, strain, and significant barriers to adaptation or development" (p. 3418). Organizations, by their nature, are unique (Mintzberg, 1979), and the mechanisms by which they build, nurture, and demonstrate resilience are also distinctive. These practices are especially critical given that organizations exist in an increasingly tightly coupled and interactively complex world where the unexpected is omnipresent and the speed with which events can amplify into disaster is always increasing (Weick & Sutcliffe, 2001; Weick et al., 1999). Sutcliffe and Vogus (2003) emphasize various factors that contribute to organizational resilience, such as broadening information processing, loosening control, and using resources (human, social, emotional, and material capital). These practices include an emphasis on enhancing continuous individual and collective learning; developing a structure to facilitate learning, skill-building, and knowledge exchange; and loosening control in a way that empowers individuals with the relevant and specific knowledge and expertise to make decisions throughout the organization. As Sutcliffe and Vogus (2003) note, an effective leader can support and cultivate collective resilience when they "foster belief in the group's conjoint capabilities" (p. 106). Furthermore, as is well documented in the research on this subject, a resilient organization is a hopeful one, insofar as it is better prepared for present challenges and more likely to build capacity for the inevitable next time (Sutcliffe & Vogus, 2003). Finally, as discussed extensively in chapter 1, the ability to learn from their experiences—both successes and failures—can help organizations to become more resilient (Kayes, 2015).

Inspiring Growth in the Aftermath of Trauma

Crisis situations threaten and often pose danger to those most impacted by the event, yet they also create opportunities for individual and collective growth. Resilience, as documented in the scholarly literature, is recognized as a key factor in not just *surviving* adversity but also *thriving* from it. The writing on post-traumatic growth expands our understanding of how individuals, teams, and organizations might experience positive change as an outcome of the adversity found in crisis situations. Importantly, post-traumatic growth is both a process and an outcome of the process of coping with challenging experiences, and it can often co-exist with an individual's experience of post-traumatic stress (Tedeschi et al., 2018). Noting that the English word "trauma" comes from the ancient Greek *trauma*, meaning "wound," Walsh (2007) offers a review of the types of loss that one might encounter when experiencing the wounds of trauma. These might be losses from the following:

- sense of physical or psychological wholeness (e.g., with serious bodily harm)
- significant persons, roles, and relationships
- head of family or community leader
- intact family unit, homes, or communities
- way of life and economic livelihood
- future potential (e.g., with the loss of children)
- hopes and dreams for all that might have been
- shattered assumptions in core worldview (e.g., loss of security, predictability, or trust). (p. 209)

Although a more comprehensive review of the biological, psychological, and social writing on trauma lies beyond the scope of this project, it is important to acknowledge the individual factors that shape one's experience and response to various situations. One person's life-changing trauma may be a temporary setback for others. This is certainly the case during organizational crises, insofar as the broader impact of such events can be felt across a community with varying effects. As Walsh (2007) summarizes, "Studies have found that the effects of trauma depend greatly on whether those wounded seek comfort, reassurance, and safety with others. Strong connections, with trust that others will be there for them when needed, counteract feelings of insecurity, helplessness, and meaninglessness. Times of great tragedy can bring out the best in the human spirit: ordinary people show extraordinary courage, compassion, and generosity in helping kin, neighbors, and strangers to recover and rebuild lives" (p. 208).

The positive change that might result from traumatic events extends across five domains: (1) emergence of new opportunities and possibilities, (2) deeper relationships and greater compassion for others, (3) feeling strengthened to meet future life challenges, (4) reordered priorities and fuller appreciation of life, and (5) deepening spirituality (Calhoun & Tedeschi, 1999, 2006; Tedeschi & Calhoun, 1995). Furthermore, the changes one might encounter when experiencing post-traumatic growth occur in three ways: (1) perceived changes in self, (2) changes in one's relationships with others, and (3) a changed philosophy of life. Following a crisis or an otherwise traumatic event, those impacted by the event may feel more confident in their ability to handle stressful situations, may develop a deeper appreciation for their existing relationships, or may recognize new practices, experiences, or innovations from which they can grow because of the adverse event. As depicted in table 2, Cunningham and Pfeiffer (2022) offer key questions associated with each of these empirically derived post-traumatic growth domains (Tedeschi et al., 2017), along with additional considerations for each domain as described by R. C. Wilson et al. (2022) and Ramos and Leal (2012).

As Walsh (2007) writes, "Resilience involves 'mastering the possible,' coming to accept what has been lost and cannot be changed, while directing efforts to what can be done and seizing opportunities for something good to come out of the tragedy" (p. 213). This shift in perspective gets to the core of what Dweck (2008) characterizes as a growth mindset. Individuals with a fixed mindset tend to view ability as static and constantly being evaluated, whereas those with a growth mindset recognize the dynamic and changeable nature of ability that is cultivated and nurtured through effort and perseverance (Dweck, 2008). In relation to adversity, such as the kind one might experience during times of crisis, such experiences may challenge one's sense of self—or, from a growth mindset perspective, these crucible moments can provide opportunities for learning, flourishing, and growth. The FIRST

TABLE 2 Domains of Post-traumatic Growth: Key Questions and Considerations

New possibilities	What new ideas have you developed because of your traumatic experience(s)? What new practices, experiences, and innovations have you, your community, your family, or your team developed in response to your trauma(s)?	Through reflection on the traumatic event, we may recognize new possibilities or opportunities in life that had never been considered prior to the event.
Relating to others	Of your current and past relationships, which ones have become stronger or closer since your experience with trauma(s)?	When we seek support from family and friends and are vulnerable as we share the impact of our trauma, we gain a stronger appreciation and connection with these family and friends.
Personal strength	How have your perceived certain strengths increased because of the trauma(s) you have experienced or are experiencing?	After reflecting on the trauma and our process growing through it, we recognize opportunities for growth and change behaviors.
Appreciation of life	Do you see life differently now that you have experienced or are experiencing trauma(s)? Are there aspects of your life that you no longer take for granted?	When we reflect on a trauma and identify the smaller things in life that were unimportant before the traumatic experience, we now have greater value in the larger scheme of life.
Spiritual change	Because of your past or ongoing trauma(s), how have your spiritual, existential, or nonspiritual views changed? What aspects of growth do you personally assess on the basis of these changes?	After experiencing a traumatic event, we may feel a stronger pull toward spirituality as a strategy for growth.

SOURCES: Cunningham & Pfeiffer (2022); Ramos & Leal (2012); Tedeschi et al. (2017); R. C. Wilson et al. (2022).

model introduced by Alvarez-Robinson (2024) proves to be a useful one for building individual and collective resilience during times of adversity and to building a growth mindset in response to these critical incidents. Writing of the various applications to higher education, the model consists of the following components:

1. Find your locus of control.
2. Investigate and manage your fear.
3. Reprogramme negative and defeatist thinking.
4. Seek healthy support.
5. Take time for self-care.

These challenging moments often serve as catalysts for personal and professional achievement, and they help to crystallize the tenacity, resolve, courage—and the individual and collective resilience—that are often viewed as markers of success (Dweck, 2008; Koehn, 2018). As Bennis and Thomas (2002) write, "One of the most reliable indicators and predictors of true leadership is an individual's ability to find meaning in negative events and to learn from even the most trying circumstances. Put another way, the skills required to conquer adversity and emerge stronger and more committed than ever are the same ones that make for extraordinary leaders" (p. 39).

The concepts of resilience, specifically CTR and organizational resilience, and post-traumatic growth are relevant to the scope of this book for myriad reasons. Within the context of crisis, resilient organizations are more likely to withstand the pressures of the moment and rebound from adversity by becoming more resourceful and with greater strength. Viewed through the lens of CTR, resilience is understood to be a process that is constituted through communication, rather than a trait that some individuals within the organization possess—or fail to possess. This is especially important for decentralized organizations, such as colleges and universities, that experience crisis, in which influence is distributed, decision making is dispersed, and the ability to recover is dependent upon the interactions, relationships, and strength of the collective. In such systems, leadership in the aftermath of crisis must also be distributed, dispersed, and cognizant of the interactions across the whole. In the aftermath of crisis, therefore, the focus should center not on whether an individual or organization is or is not resilient, but rather on the ways in which leaders can help to cultivate and reinforce the resilience of the community. Furthermore, as explored in the examples to follow, effective leadership practices across higher education can help to cultivate resilience and inspire growth in the aftermath of tragedy.

Higher Education Applications

With a grounding in the resilience and post-traumatic growth literature, we can now consider how these practices might play out across colleges and universities. Empirical studies exploring the dynamics of crisis are increasingly published in higher education, leadership, communication, and other related fields. In drawing upon the lessons learned across a wide range of cases, resilience often emerges as a central theme. For example, as Fernandez et al. (2022) found in their analysis of the University of Houston's response to Hurricane Ike in September 2018 and Hurricane Harvey in August 2017, university administrators exercised resilience by taking time to communicate and process information, use material resources, and model compassion through the extension of emotional or relational resources. Other studies point to the potential for resilience and post-traumatic growth among higher education stakeholders in response to natural disasters (Ayebi-Arthur, 2017; Kaye-Kauderer et al., 2020), mass violence and mass shootings (Mancini et al., 2016; Miron et al., 2014; Nucifora et al., 2007), and acts of racial unrest (Chhikara et al., 2022; Cole et al., 2021; Sanchez et al., 2022). Each of these types of crises pose operational and reputational risks for the institution, demand careful planning and coordination, and require immediate attention from university administrators. Furthermore, they each uniquely threaten the perceived sense of safety and well-being within the institution. Finally, in addition to these examples of research on post-crisis resilience in higher education, resilience is also referred to as a protective factor in promoting leadership development for underrepresented minorities and women during adverse crucible experiences (Ledesma, 2014; Lewis-Strickland, 2021; Pillay-Naidoo & Nel, 2022).

We are also seeing a flurry of scholarly research exploring the manifestations of resilience and post-traumatic growth across colleges and universities as a result of the COVID-19 pandemic (Bozkurt, 2022; Calcado et al., 2022; Gigliotti, 2020, 2021; McNamara, 2021; Nandy et al., 2021; Ruben, 2020; Shaya et al., 2022). Denney (2021) goes so far as to advocate for compassionate leadership during this post-pandemic period, adding an emphasis on the need for courage and resilience. She writes the following on the centrality of resilience: "Resilience is about understanding where our breaking points are, and stopping well before them. Resilience is about experiencing disappointment or failure, reflecting on this and responding to it stronger than before. Resilience, to me, is a collective community responsibility, where all members of a community should come together to understand what is broken in a system and agree on ways in which it can be made better—and this is how our university leadership can demonstrate and build resilience in individuals and in the community" (p. 47).

In a research brief published by Excelencia in Education, an organization focused on Latino student success, the authors detail the resilience of five Puerto Rican Hispanic-serving institutions in responding to a series of crises, including Hurricanes Irma and Maria, earthquakes, unexpected changes in governmental leadership, demographic shifts, and the COVID-19 pandemic (Santiago et al., 2023). As the authors suggest, these incidents "tested the spirit, structure, and sustainability of communities and institutions serving them in Puerto Rico" (p. 6). The authors go on to describe various strategies that contributed to the resilience of these institutions, including the merger of campuses and services; the reimagination of recruitment, enrollment, and retention strategies; the restructure of institutional finances; and the redesign of program offerings (Santiago et al., 2023). The four priorities that served as a guide during this period of prolonged crisis included (1) sustaining institutional management, (2) managing enrollment plans and expectations, (3) supporting students by meeting their basic needs and providing wraparound services, and (4) preparing students for graduation and post-completion (Santiago et al., 2023, p. 5).

I had an opportunity to interview senior leaders across higher education to explore their perceptions of crisis and their experiences in leading units, departments, and institutions through various types of crises (see Gigliotti, 2019). The findings from that study informed my thinking on crisis leadership and the need for pursuing a values-based and communication-oriented paradigm of crisis leadership in higher education. A number of key insights gleaned from that research center on these themes of resilience and growth—and the role leaders can play in helping to further cultivate an environment where resilience and growth are made possible in the aftermath of crisis. One particularly poignant case involved the child sex abuse scandal at Pennsylvania State University (Penn State) and the resilience of the community that allowed the organization to move forward.

CULTIVATING RESILIENCE IN THE AFTERMATH OF THE JERRY SANDUSKY SCANDAL

State College, Pennsylvania, is frequently cited as one of the best college towns in the United States and is home to the flagship campus of Penn State University, University Park. National and international media outlets flooded the bucolic college town following the release of a 2011 grand jury report and subsequent arrest of Jerry Sandusky, an assistant coach for the Penn State Nittany Lions football team, for alleged child sexual abuse over a period of fifteen years. The grand jury report accused Sandusky of using the charity he initially founded in 1977, Second Mile, to identify, befriend, and ultimately abuse young boys, "many of whom were vulnerable due to their social situations" (Thirty-Third Statewide Investigating Grand Jury, p. 1). Some of the acts of abuse and inappropriate sexual conduct occurred on the University Park campus and in Sandusky's residence. Additionally, three Penn State officials—President Graham B. Spanier, Senior Vice President for Finance and Business Gary C. Schultz, and Athletic Director Timothy M. Curley—were charged with perjury, obstruction of justice, failure to report suspected child abuse, and related charges. On November 9, 2011, longtime head football coach, Joe Paterno, announced his intention to retire at the end of the 2011 football season. Hours later, the university's board of trustees announced the immediate firing of President Spanier and Coach Paterno. As Paterno shared in a press release to the community, "This is a tragedy. It is one of the great sorrows of my life. With the benefit of hindsight, I wish I had done more" (Viera, 2011). Viera (2011) described what took place after the board of trustees press conference as follows: "The scandal, and the fallout from it, has left Penn State's normally placid campus in a state of shock. Scores of students poured into the streets downtown in the immediate aftermath of the news conference. Many held up cellphones to take pictures and others blew vuvuzelas and air horns. A few climbed lampposts, tried to topple street signs and knocked over trash cans. Others set off firecrackers from the roofs of buildings, and a television news truck was flipped on its side. A lamppost was torn down and police pepper-sprayed some in the crowd."

The board of trustees commissioned an independent investigation by former Federal Bureau of Investigation director Louis Freeh, whose report stated that Paterno, along with Spanier, Schultz, and Curley, had known about allegations of child abuse by Sandusky as early as 1998. As documented in the Freeh report, "The most saddening finding by the Special Investigative Counsel is the total and consistent disregard by the most senior leaders at Penn State for the safety and welfare of Sandusky's child victims" (Freeh Sporkin & Sullivan LLP, 2012, p. 14). Referring to a "culture of reverence for the football program that is ingrained at all levels of the campus community," the report called for a "transformation of the culture that permitted Sandusky's behavior . . . and which directly contributed to the failure of Penn State's most powerful leaders to adequately report and respond to the actions of a serial sexual predator" (pp. 17, 18).

To date, this child sexual abuse scandal remains one of the most staggering crises to impact higher education in the United States, and it preceded a number of other high-profile sexual abuse scandals that would eventually follow at Ohio State University, Michigan State University, and the University of Michigan. A report of the sexual abuse case at Penn State indicated that the university and its insurers have spent upwards of $250 million on fees related to the crisis, with $5.3 million spent on crisis communications and other consultants alone (Johnson, 2012). The case also led to sweeping reform across the education and social services landscape in order to improve child protection, including changing requirements for individuals who work or volunteer with children and an increasing number of mandated reporters who are required to report any Title IX violations to the university as soon as possible.

To better understand the dynamics of crisis leadership in higher education, I conducted interviews with nearly forty senior leaders across various colleges and universities in 2016. The full report of these findings appears in Gigliotti (2019). The focus on resilience was pervasive in all of the interviews I conducted with senior officials from Penn State. As one individual noted,

> If there's one thing that defines Penn State historically, both
> before and after the crisis, it's a strong sense of community, a
> strong kinship to the institution. Yeah, I think everybody has
> their institutional loyalties, whether it's Rutgers, whether it's
> Michigan or Ohio State, or whatever. Students and alums feel
> very passionate about their alma mater. It just seems like it's
> raised to a different level of magnitude here. There was just,

I think, bewilderment is a good term. People felt quite a bit like they had been taken into a dark alley and pummeled and had all of their convictions about a place they thought they knew very, very well turned upside down in a very short span of time. It was very, I think to the whole community, very unsettling.

This sentiment was reflected in an announcement shared with alumni, friends, and benefactors of Penn State in the immediate aftermath of the crisis, inviting the community to retain their trust and support in the university during a time of unprecedented challenge:

> As one of Penn State's most generous supporters and most loyal alumni and friends, you have demonstrated extraordinary faith in this University and its future, and I know that faith was challenged by the tragic news of this week. The Board of Trustees has made difficult first steps toward helping Penn State to emerge from this crisis as a better, stronger, and prouder institution. One of those steps has been the appointment of Rodney A. Erickson, executive vice president and provost, as interim president. Dr. Erickson shared the following message with the Penn State community this morning. I would like to share it with you as well and ask you to support Dr. Erickson as he begins to lead Penn State on a path toward renewed national standing and respect.

Many individuals with whom I spoke discussed the "sense of community" that was cultivated at an institution like Penn State. As one person noted, unlike many other college campuses across the country, "people come here and there aren't other, I don't want to say distractions, but there aren't other temptations. . . . You're here and it's a pretty captive audience and you really get cemented to the institution. It is a lot, it's about sports, but it's a lot more. . . . People, I think, come here and get immersed and get bonded to the place." Another senior leader described this feature of the institution as a source of its resilience:

> This is the only land-grant university in the Commonwealth. The scale and scope of Penn State in serving a wide swath of the population is impressive, and inclusive of serving a lot of first-generation, hard-working students who go on to accomplish great things with grit and determination. There is something special about the sense of community that's cultivated particularly through University Park. There's I imagine some combination of history and geographic location, even isolation, that helped to account for some of those things. There's definitely something in the water here that people point to. One of those strengths is the strength of community and work ethic. People don't get rocked.

In support of this depiction of strength and the ability to withstand the pressures of a crisis of this magnitude, one senior officer provided rich insight into the dynamics of resilience that allowed the institution to recover:

> I have used [the term *resilience*] quite often to describe Penn State in the wake of the crisis. What might be the one term that would best characterize the entire institutional response, not just the administration, not just the governing board, but the students, faculty, staff, and alums. I would say that the term resilience is that term that is most apt as a single descriptor of how the institution responded. That's not to say, again, that there aren't things that to this day continue to rend the community, notwithstanding the differences of opinion about what Joe Paterno's proper legacy should be or Graham Spanier's proper legacy should be. There's still, the one thing that pulls the community together is this abiding affection in and belief of Penn State, belief in Penn State, and that everybody is

energetically working toward that objective of getting the institution dusted off, picked up, and back on its feet as quickly as possible.

When I think about the fact that we sustained a credit rating downgrade from Moody's within a year after the indictments were handed down, and then just recently this spring, we're elevated back to AA1. . . . When you know, as I do, that credit ratings aren't just reflections of financial performance, but they're looking at philanthropy, they're looking at your enrollment demand, they're looking at your research income, they're looking at basically all the key facets that describe a university's health and well-being. The resiliency that we've seen, I don't have any frame of reference for it because I just in my life. . . . Yeah, I've experienced tough times, tough challenges, yes, and even a few crises, but never anything as dramatically big as what happened to Penn State and never kind of the bounce-back phenomenon that we've seen in the span of really four short years.

Reinforcing the resilience of the community, another senior leader noted the following: "We underestimate I think how resilient we are, each as individuals, or as an institution is, I feel we're tested. There are lots of people that rise to the occasion when they have to. We saw that at Penn State. While it was the most difficult time in my career, it also provided the most rewarding and meaningful moments in my career, just because of some of the really fine things that happened when we felt really under siege."

The child abuse scandal and subsequent fallout at Penn State provide a vivid glimpse into the inherent tragedy of crisis—and the important role resilience can play in helping members of a community withstand and recover from the pressures of the moment. Of course, any consideration of a case of this kind must also note the devastating and long-lasting impact on the direct victims of Sandusky's sexual abuse, and the hope that they too will experience resilience and appropriate healing in the aftermath of such trauma.

Beyond the description of resilience shared by university senior leaders at Penn State and the various metrics indicating a return to near-normal operations in the aftermath of the sexual abuse crisis, Eury et al. (2018) provide additional empirical data regarding the resilience of the community and the durability of their sense of attachment and identification to the institution. In their comprehensive analysis of 25,335 communications from 14,309 alumni sent to various university offices from November 2011 to December 2012, the authors describe the importance of "legacy identification," such that alumni continue to define themselves in terms of the organization's ideals and values, even upon graduation from the institution. The authors describe the impact of legacy identification in serving "as a reservoir from which members draw during identification threats, and also provides a way to compare past with present, past with future, and present with future. In this sense, it can provide either a sense of identity continuity (continuing on as before) or discontinuity (changing the character of one's identification)" (pp. 835, 836). As the authors note, "We found that alumni drew upon their legacy identification as they went through an emotion-laden struggle involving predominantly positive experiences in the past, predominantly negative experiences in the present, and uncertain experiences in the future" (p. 826).

In conclusion, we might consider the special issue of the *Penn Stater*, the alumni association's magazine, that was published in January 2012, and what it means for this story of post-crisis resilience. The black cover depicted a fallen jumble of letters at the bottom of the page forming "Penn State," next to the simple tag, "Our darkest days." The special issue featured sections on child sex abuse, how something like this could have happened at Penn State, what it means to be a Penn Stater, and the role of alumni going forward (Frantz, 2012). The magazine also included letters from alumni expressing outrage and support for the victims, and in some cases, support for Coach Paterno (Frantz, 2012). As editor Tiny Hay described in an interview with the *Patriot-News*, "From the get-go, we wanted to be thoughtful . . . and reflective and not hasty and hysterical. We wanted to contend with what people were reading in the most extreme news media." The resilience that emerged during these "darkest days" appeared to come from the unique conditions of the Penn State community and a history of building durable relationships with students, alumni, and employees. In the spirit of a CRT orientation, resilience was cultivated communicatively and collectively, and the case may serve as a guide for other leaders and institutions seeking to draw upon this resilience during times of prolonged and shocking distress. Furthermore, moving beyond this focus on the crisis at Penn State, other types of crises detailed in later chapters of this book, including institutional responses to the COVID-19 pandemic and the responses to national incidents of racial injustice, paint a similar picture of higher education leaders seeking to draw upon the resilience of their communities in responding meaningfully to institutional and national moments of reckoning.

Considerations for Post-Crisis Leadership Action

Certainly, colleges and universities must exercise a high degree of responsibility to prevent crises such as the one detailed in this chapter from occurring again. Leaders of these institutions also serve an important role in helping to build, restore, and accentuate the resilience of the community in the aftermath of crisis. Several actions might prove advantageous in cultivating resilience during this critical post-crisis phase:

- Pay attention to the dynamic process of resilience and the ways in which members of one's unit, department, or organization can bounce back or reintegrate with confidence and conviction.
- Devote attention to issues related to equity and inclusion. Be mindful of the often disproportionate impact of crises on individuals and units and the ways in which you can best support and nurture the resilience of those adversely affected by the crisis.

- Be aware of your resilience narrative. Engage in communication that reinforces the resilience of the community and that highlights the areas of strength, distinction, and hope that are made manifest during times of crisis.
- Lean on colleagues throughout the institution and across other organizations for support and strength. Leadership is not a solo endeavor, and the ability to rely on the assistance of others can prove to be an asset for leaders during times of despair and uncertainty.
- Be wary of compassion fatigue and prioritize your own self-care. As suggested by Field (2020), "You can't take care of others if you don't take care of yourself. People who are managing crises have to take time to clear their mind and re-energize, so they can continue to do the work they have to do."
- Accept the inherent vulnerability associated with loss or trauma—and forge a path forward that is grounded in optimism that can help to transcend this vulnerability.
- Do not underestimate the value of adopting positive emotions. In their research on the impact of positive emotions experienced in the wake of the September 11 attacks, Fredrickson et al. (2003) found that positive emotions in the aftermath of crises buffer resilient people against depression and fuel thriving. As the authors note, "Subtle and fleeting experiences of gratitude, interest, love, and other positive emotions appeared to hold depressive symptoms at bay and fuel postcrisis growth" (p. 374).
- Model transformational leadership behaviors that align with your authentic style and that best meet the moment. These behaviors include idealized influence, inspirational motivation, intellectual stimulation, and individualized consideration (Bass, 1985, 1998). As Sommer et al. (2016) found in their empirical study of 426 team members and 52 leaders conducted in the midst of an organizational crisis in health care, both positive and negative affect can co-exist within individuals confronting a crisis. In a crisis, transformational leadership behaviors were associated with higher levels of positive affect and lower levels of negative

affect among team members, which in turn predicted higher resilience among team members.

- Support the process of post-traumatic growth. As Koloroutis and Pole (2021) describe, such a process "is facilitated by leaders who are present, understand trauma and trauma responses, and can listen to and support individuals and teams by meeting them exactly where they are" (p. 30).

- Engage in reflective practice. R. C. Wilson et al. (2022) advocate for leaders to prioritize time for reflection as a mechanism for nurturing personal, professional, and post-traumatic growth. As the authors indicate, "Reflection is a nourishing practice that deepens our compassion and empathy toward ourselves and others" (p. 263), and it allows leaders and those they lead to grow from stress and trauma and thereby to be better prepared for whatever might lie ahead.

- Facilitate recovery in the aftermath of traumatic events by drawing upon some of the suggestions advanced by Walsh and McGoldrick (2004):
  - Engage in an empathic and shared acknowledgment of the reality of the traumatic event. Clarify any facts, circumstances, or ambiguities.
  - Recognize the shared experience of loss and survivorship. Actively participate in any memorial rituals, tributes, or rites of passage that may accompany such events.
  - Plan for the well-being of survivors and those most directly affected by the crisis.
  - Reinvest in relationships.

- Explore ways of strengthening the resilience of your unit, department, or institution. For example, consider the items in Wagnild and Young's (1993) resilience scale depicted in table 3, and adopt tailored strategies to bolster individual and collective resilience in anticipation of future periods of adversity.

The resilience modeled by individuals and teams can have a dramatic impact on how they respond to and recover from a crisis.

TABLE 3 The 25-Item Resilience Scale

CODE	ITEM
IRS_1	When I make plans, I follow through with them.
IRS_2	I usually manage one way or another.
IRS_3	I am able to depend on myself more than anyone else.
IRS_4	Keeping interested in things is important to me.
IRS_5	I can be on my own if I have to.
IRS_6	I feel proud that I have accomplished things in life.
IRS_7	I usually take things in stride.
IRS_8	I am friends with myself.
IRS_9	I feel that I can handle many things at a time.
IRS_10	I am determined.
IRS_11	I seldom wonder what the point of it all is.
IRS_12	I take things one day at a time.
IRS_13	I can get through difficult times because I've experienced difficulty before.
IRS_14	I have self-discipline.
IRS_15	I keep interested in things.
IRS_16	I can usually find something to laugh about.
IRS_17	My belief in myself gets me through hard times.
IRS_18	In an emergency, I'm someone people can generally rely on.
IRS_19	I can usually look at a situation in a number of ways.
IRS_20	Sometimes I make myself do things whether I want to or not.
IRS_21	My life has meaning.
IRS_22	I do not dwell on things that I can't do anything about.
IRS_23	When I'm in a difficult situation, I can usually find my way out of it.
IRS_24	I have enough energy to do what I have to do.
IRS_25	It's okay if there are people who don't like me.

SOURCE: Wagnild & Young (1993, p. 169).

As reflected by these suggestions and the supporting literature and examples detailed in this chapter, those engaged in post-crisis leadership can help to cultivate individual and collective resilience. The capacity to bounce back—or bounce forward—following a crisis also relies on one's ability to derive meaning and purpose from events that are often characterized as overwhelming, disorienting, and senseless. This is the focus of attention to which we now turn.

3

Stimulate Meaning-Making

Crises are often destabilizing events in the life of any organization. These incidents have the potential to disrupt what members have come to expect and accept as normal, threatening both the values and core operations of an organization and impacting its security, well-being, and sense of community. As Sellnow and Seeger (2020) write, "These events shatter the fundamental sense of normalcy, stability, and predictability we all count on in living our daily lives" (p. 17). Although some crises may be anticipated, these shocking and intense events often come as a surprise to members of a community, leaving people blindsided and jolted by the acute shock they cause. Weick (1993) describes such events as cosmology episodes, which occur "when people suddenly and deeply feel that the universe is no longer a rational, orderly system. What makes such an episode so shattering is that both the sense of what is occurring and the means to rebuild that sense collapse together" (p. 633). At such times, the ground on which one stands can seem shaken and unsteady and may lead to confusion about who to lean on for support during a period of profound instability. These events often result in overwhelming sadness, despair, fear, and uncertainty, and the sudden loss of meaning associated with such events demands leadership attention. This chapter will take a closer look at the role of post-crisis leadership in helping to make meaning of these shocking, troubling, and yet often inevitable occurrences, and will draw upon some of the relevant communication scholarship related to sensemaking, framing, and the management of meaning as a guide for applied post-crisis leadership.

The Search for Meaning

Meaning is embedded in our individual lived experiences, and the ways in which we create and derive meaning from these experiences will vary throughout the course of our lives. The highs and lows that we encounter over a lifetime provide unique opportunities for meaning-making. Indeed, these periods of extreme joy and distress help to punctuate a life and serve as important markers in the stories that are told and retold over time. The act of finding meaning involves a process of narrative construction—and these narratives help to bring coherence and order to people's experiences. Consider, for example, the ways in which individuals depict key milestones from their life story, such as in sharing news of the birth and death of loved ones, the peaks and valleys associated with their professional journey, and the decline and regrowth that they may experience in relationship with others. The narrative becomes a by-product or outcome of their meaning-making experience—and it is this narrative that is shared and reshared in our attempts to co-construct reality with others.

As crucible moments in the life of an organization and its members, the volatility and uncertainty attributed to crises contribute to the cultivation of a dynamic laboratory from which to understand and analyze the conditions of meaning-making. The adversity, loss, or trauma associated with crises can test individual and collective character. The emotions that might accompany such events—fear, distress, or uncertainty—have the potential to stall or problematize meaning-making efforts. For example, a crisis may jolt someone's sense of security or well-being and may cause them to call into question previously held assumptions. Given the inevitability of crisis, the following questions become useful for those seeking to find meaning during these periods of turbulence:

- How does one engage in meaning-making during the times of crisis, suffering, and despair that are an inevitable part of the human condition?
- How can one find meaning when the ground upon which one stands seems to be crumbling?
- What possibilities for individual and collective transformation are embedded in crisis events or situations?
- To what extent might those engaged in leadership help support others in making sense of seemingly senseless times and assist others in their search for purpose, fulfillment, or resolve during these difficult seasons of their life?

In his story of survival based on his three years in Auschwitz and other Nazi concentration camps, Frankl (1992) turns often to the words of Nietzsche that "he who has a *why* to live can bear with almost any *how*." Many of the crises to befall institutions of higher education, and the converging environmental challenges that provide a backdrop for this analysis, can lead to a great deal of pain, loss, and suffering. The insights shared in Frankl's text help to situate the dynamics of meaning-making in response to such suffering. Questioning that which makes life meaningful and purposeful, Frankl writes: "If there is meaning in life at all, then there must be meaning in suffering. Suffering is an ineradicable part of life, even as fate and death. Without suffering and death human life cannot be complete. . . . In some way, suffering ceases to be suffering at the moment it finds meaning" (pp. 76, 117).

Frankl goes on to note that this sense of meaning differs "from man to man, and from moment to moment" (p. 85). We are reminded often of individuals who turn moments of personal tragedy and tribulation into triumph, even when dealing with events that are widely viewed as dire, hopeless, and senseless. One's personal meaning always remains in flux; however, as Frankl reminds us, it never ceases to be. In introducing his psychological theory of logotherapy, he presents three pathways through which one might discover meaning: "(1) by creating a work or doing a deed, (2) by experiencing something or encountering someone, and (3) by the attitude we take toward unavoidable suffering" (p. 115).

The search for meaning is a topic of widespread interest, especially given the ongoing pressures facing individuals and communities across the globe. In a 2021 study of seventeen advanced economies conducted by the Pew Research Center, the data highlight the ways in which people draw meaning and fulfillment from the activities that constitute their daily lives (see figure 2). As the authors of the study describe, "This is particularly the case when it comes to people's occupations and careers, which are a top-three source of meaning in many publics" (Silver et al., 2021, para. 1). Family was found to be the top source of meaning in life for most of the publics surveyed. Beyond work and family, "some people—particularly older adults—find meaning in the absence of work, retirement. People also rely on their personal hobbies, education, volunteer work, and travel for a sense of purpose, referencing everything from listening to music to international trips" (Silver at al., 2021, para. 1).

The potential for human suffering or death is a risk that accompanies many types of organizational crises. For some, the loss of life is what might very well differentiate a crisis from a noncrisis. In the spirit of better understanding how some individuals may find meaning during these times of potential suffering, we might consider the practice of memento mori, a Latin phrase meaning "remember your death." In an article about this practice in the *New York Times*, Sister Theresa Aletheia Noble from the Daughters of Saint Paul Convent describes her attempt to revive this spiritual practice of purposeful and daily consideration of one's death (Graham, 2021). The custom of regular meditation on death is one that extends across religious and spiritual

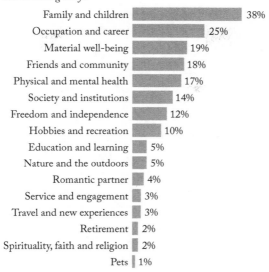

Family, careers and material well-being are among the most cited factors for what makes life meaningful

Median % who mention—when describing what gives them meaning in life

Family and children	38%
Occupation and career	25%
Material well-being	19%
Friends and community	18%
Physical and mental health	17%
Society and institutions	14%
Freedom and independence	12%
Hobbies and recreation	10%
Education and learning	5%
Nature and the outdoors	5%
Romantic partner	4%
Service and engagement	3%
Travel and new experiences	3%
Retirement	2%
Spirituality, faith and religion	2%
Pets	1%

FIG. 2. Factors associated with a meaningful life (Pew Research Center, 2021).

traditions. As described in the article, the practice of memento mori allows one to "intentionally think about your own death every day, as a means of appreciating the present and focusing on the future. It can seem radical in an era in which death—until very recently—has become easy to ignore" (Graham, 2021). Suffering and death—both of which may accompany crises—are an inevitable part of the human experience. For Sister Aletheia, "focusing only on the 'bright and shiny' is superficial and inauthentic. 'We try to suppress the thought of death, or escape it, or run away from it because we think that's where we'll find happiness,' she said. 'But it's actually in facing the darkest realities of life that we find light in them'" (Graham, 2021). As she wrote in her journal, "Remembering death keeps us awake, focused, and ready for whatever might happen—both the excruciatingly difficult and the breathtakingly beautiful" (Graham, 2021).

To be sure, just because death and suffering are inevitable elements of the human condition, to experience such hardship during times of crisis—especially those that are viewed as preventable—can be hard to accept and should never be taken for granted. And of course, it is incumbent on colleges and universities and their leadership teams to take appropriate measures to protect the safety and well-being of all members of their community and to minimize the potential for any harm. However, despite even the very best preparation and prevention efforts, the loss of life and the potential for distress can come to be expected for institutions the size of small- and medium-sized cities.

Seeger and Sellnow (2016) describe the ways in which crises disrupt individual, group, community, and social meaning. As they explain, these episodes "alter a sense of personal identity, create a sense of dislocation and disorientation, and disrupt established notions of personal significance. They may change strongly held beliefs about the world—what is important and what might be considered dangerous and risky. They disrupt established life narratives but create new ones" (p. 47). It is through communication that leaders can help others make sense of such episodes, and this communication includes the stories one shares, the symbols one invokes, and the strategies one pursues in describing the larger lessons from such events. Leaders play an important role in helping to encourage and stimulate meaning-making efforts in the aftermath of crisis, and such efforts are made possible through communication—including through the core activities of sensemaking, sensegiving, framing, and the management of meaning, each of which are discussed in the sections to follow.

Sensemaking and Sensegiving

Humans live in a world of gaps, and the way we bridge those gaps reflects what is known as the act of *sensemaking* (Dervin, 1992, 1998). Sensemaking allows individuals to "structure the unknown" (Waterman, 1990, p. 41) as a way of constructing that which then becomes sensible to others (Weick, 1995). According to Weick (1995), sensemaking is the process of social construction that occurs when discrepant cues interrupt individuals' ongoing activity. It involves the retrospective development of plausible meanings that rationalize individual behaviors, and the process of sensemaking helps to make sensible and coherent the events, incidents, and actions that constitute our lived experience (Weick, 1995). During times of institutional and environmental turbulence, those engaged in leadership are called upon to engage in and stimulate sensemaking efforts. The theory of sensemaking centers on the ways that crises are *enacted* rather than *encountered*, whereby people generate the environment through their actions and meaning-making activities (Weick, 1988). Characterized by their low probability and high consequence, crises place significant demands on sensemaking. During these profoundly disruptive moments and in their aftermath, as summarized by Maitlis and Sonenshein (2010), "crises unfold through the meanings that are made of seemingly unconnected and even inconsequential events, and how these meanings often derive from a range of different [stakeholders]" (pp. 553, 554). Sensemaking occurs at both the individual and collective levels, and shared meanings can arise through social processes (Maitlis & Sonenshein, 2010).

Weick (1995) identifies seven properties of sensemaking; it is (1) a process that is grounded in identity construction, (2) retrospective, (3) enactive of sensible environments, (4) social, (5) ongoing, (6) focused on and by extracted cues, and (7) driven by plausibility rather than accuracy (p. 17). Just as leaders create their own environments, these environments shape leaders, leadership decisions, and leadership possibilities. In order to make sense of uncertain and unpredictable organizational circumstances, for example, the impetus often lies with the leader to bracket and punctuate past events—or, as Weick (1995) describes the process, to "create breaks in the stream and impose categories on those portions that are set apart. When people bracket, they act as if there is something out there to be discovered" (p. 35). This communicative process of enactment, along with sensemaking as a whole, often influences the direction of organizational events (Weick, 1988). In his analysis of organizational crises, for example, Weick (1988) suggests, "The less adequate the sensemaking process directed at a crisis, the more likely it is that the crisis will get out of control" (p. 305). Crises demand immediate attention, and these initial attempts at sensemaking can have cascading implications on how the crisis response and post-crisis recovery unfold.

The process of sensemaking involves more than interpretation. According to Weick (1995), "Sensemaking is about authoring as well as interpretation, creation as well as discovery" (p. 8). This act of interpretation and discovery allows leaders to collaborate with followers in the co-construction of meaning. Put another way, sensemaking *and* sensegiving are often at play in leader-follower interactions. The dual role of author and creator captures the leader's role in helping to make sense of and then share this sense in ways that resonate with others (Ruben & Gigliotti, 2019, 2021). The following passage by Thayer (1988) further illustrates a view of the leader as sensemaker and sensegiver:

> [A leader is] one who alters or guides the manner in which his followers "mind" the world by giving it a compelling "face."
> A leader at work is one who gives others a different sense of the *meaning* of that which they do by recreating it in a different form, a different "face," in the same way that a pivotal painter or sculptor or poet gives those who follow him (or her) a different way of "seeing"—and therefore saying and doing and knowing in the world. A leader does not tell it "as it is"; he tells it as it *might be*, giving what "is" thereby a different "face." . . . The leader is a sense-*giver*. The leader always *embodies* the possibilities of escape from what might otherwise appear to us to be incomprehensible, or from what might otherwise appear to us to be a chaotic, indifferent, or incorrigible world—one over which we have no ultimate control. (pp. 250, 254)

Leadership behaviors, actions, and words are ascribed special and symbolic meaning (Alvesson & Sveningsson, 2003), and "rather than making sense of an ambiguous situation for [oneself]," leaders play an important role in helping to make sense for others (Gioia & Chittipeddi, 1991, p. 443). Both sensemaking and sensegiving are critical leadership activities during times of change and stability (Bartunek et al., 1999; Corley & Gioia, 2004; Dunford & Jones, 2000; Gioia & Chittipeddi, 1991; Gioia et al., 1994; Maitlis & Lawrence, 2007)—and these efforts take on heightened levels of significance during and following times of crisis.

Sensemaking does not stop at the conclusion of a critical incident. In their writing on sensemaking in the aftermath of extreme events, Dwyer et al. (2023) found that sensemaking "continues as practitioners continue to try and make sense of the incident in its immediate aftermath, as they engage with the subsequent inquiry, and as they implement its recommendations" (p. 422). The authors describe the ways in which individuals engage in post-incident sensemaking and the diverse emotions that can arise as individuals draw upon various coping strategies, including fear, sadness, anger, apathy, and satisfaction. Informed by their interviews with emergency management practitioners following catastrophic bushfires in Australia that resulted in the loss of 173 lives and an estimated $4 billion in damage in 2009, Dwyer et al. (2023) note the following: "We found that interviewees associated *fear* and *sadness* with the Black Saturday incident and its immediate aftermath. They linked *anger* to the inquiry and connected *apathy* and *satisfaction* to implementation [of inquiry recommendations]. Interviewees also gave accounts of feeling worried and concerned, which we label *anxiety*, which arises when something that was previously familiar loses its meaning" (p. 429). In their coding of the interview data, the authors differentiated the coping mechanisms employed in the aftermath of the crisis from the emotions that resulted after the incident, during the inquiry, and throughout implementation.

One final point related to sensemaking and sensegiving deserves mention. It is through the communicative activities of sensemaking and sensegiving that individuals engaged in the co-construction of leadership help to render meaningful those incidents or situations that are seemingly senseless. By stimulating sensemaking efforts and in helping individuals craft meaning out of these dizzying and disorienting experiences, leaders have the potential to influence the ways in which others view, understand, accept, and find purpose in the crisis. Despite the importance of leaders in this process, it is vital to acknowledge the meaning-making process as a jointly constructed activity. As a collaborative and co-constructed endeavor, leadership is made possible through the interactions of leaders, followers, and contextual variables—and similarly, one's ability to find meaning in the aftermath of crisis is not limited to the sensemaking of leaders. Rather, meaning-making in the aftermath of crisis is socially constructed, and an understanding of this dynamic requires a broader consideration of the intersection of leaders, followers, and situation (Allen et al., 2016; Kellerman, 2016). As noted by Grint (2005), contingency theories of leadership that isolate the leader, followers, and context are inherently limited, and he calls for more attention to be paid "to the role of leaders and decision-makers in the construction of contexts that legitimates their intended or executed actions and accounts" (p. 1472). Or, as explained by Ruben and Gigliotti (2019, 2021) in their description of leadership resonance theory, one might take account of the reciprocal influence of leader and follower in the enactment and construction of leadership. Followers, or members of a community impacted by crises, will often take their cue based on how formal and informal leaders choose to frame certain events or situations. Referring to concepts described by Frankl (1992), Walsh (2007) offers a reminder that "in recovery work, we may need to help people reconstruct a new sense of normality, identity, and relatedness to adapt to altered conditions. We cannot make meaning for them; our task is to support their efforts" (p. 211).

Framing and the Management of Meaning

As Fairhurst and Sarr (1996) write in the introduction to their book *The Art of Framing: Managing the Language of Leadership*, "Leaders operate in uncertain, sometimes chaotic environments that are partly of their own creation: while leaders do not control events, they do influence how events are seen and understood" (p. xi). Leaders are perceived as having the ability to co-create the contexts, situations, and opportunities upon which they and others must respond (Fairhurst, 2009). It is through the act of framing that individuals come to accept one meaning or interpretation over another. During times of volatility, uncertainty, complexity, and ambiguity (VUCA), such as during and following periods of crisis, those engaged in leadership have an obligation to frame the event or situation in ways that establish clarity, trust, confidence, and hope (Barber, 1992; A. Fletcher et al., 2023). Drawing upon the work of Pondy (1978), Entman (1993), and Weick (1979), Fairhurst and Sarr (1996) define framing as "the ability to shape the meaning of a subject, to judge its character and significance. To hold the frame of a subject is to choose one particular meaning (or set of meanings) over another. When we share our frames with others (the process of framing), we manage meaning because we assert that our interpretations should be taken as real over other possible interpretations" (p. 3).

Not only is "talk" the way in which leaders accomplish specific tasks (Gronn, 1983), but it is through communication—and framing, more specifically—that leaders help others in deriving meaning from times of chaos, confusion, and uncertainty (Fairhurst & Sarr, 1996).

One way that leaders can encourage the co-construction of meaning in the aftermath of crisis is through the use of poignant questions. Although posited by Milner and Echterling (2021) as questions for therapists to use in helping others find meaning during the COVID-19 pandemic, leaders might consider adapting similar types of questions as a way of stimulating meaning-making:

- After all that you have learned about the pandemic so far, what are the most important lessons for you?
- In what ways has your life mission changed as a result of your experience?
- What discoveries have you made about yourself during this time?
- What advice would you give someone who is struggling to find meaning in this troubled time?
- What beliefs and values have given you strength during the pandemic? (p. 301)

In addition to posing questions that can encourage meaning-making, the authors also call attention to the process of reframing. As they note, "Reframing is based on the phenomenon that by changing the context of a painting, for example, one can effect how it is perceived . . . when one views the pandemic experience in a context that also highlights courage, compassion, and coping, the story becomes one of potential triumph" (p. 302).

Framing becomes a useful leadership strategy during the period that follows a crisis. In attempting to restore some normalcy and in reminding individuals of the potential learning opportunities embedded in the crisis, discursive framing tactics can help members of a community embrace new possibilities that might result from the crisis. Furthermore, the ways in which the event is framed can influence short-term and long-term responses to any given crisis. As James and Wooten (2022) write, "The way we frame a situation, and how we outline its dimensions in our own minds, affects the way we make decisions about what to do in that situation" (p. 45). Referring to conceptualizations of crises as threats and opportunities, the authors go on to describe the importance of how we subjectively choose to frame these inherently ambiguous events and situations: "For most of us, crises are predominantly threats. We are inclined to frame them as a danger—to ourselves, our people, our organizations, and our stakeholders. But crises are *ambiguous*. They are both threats *and* opportunities. Yet how you navigate a crisis and how you respond to its threats and its opportunities in your decision-making depends very much on the subjective frame you use" (p. 45).

Crises are disruptive, shocking, and intense events, and making sense of them and re-establishing some degree of normalcy in their aftermath requires communication. This is certainly the case for the types of crises to befall institutions of higher education described in this book. Facing a barrage of institutional and environmental pressures, college and university leaders often find themselves providing this management-of-meaning function—and we can draw upon some of these public examples in order to better understand some of the ways in which the concepts introduced in this chapter find real-life applications in the practice of post-crisis leadership. As detailed in the examples outlined below, elements of sensemaking, sensegiving, framing, and management of meaning are clearly represented in the official communication regarding institutional planning and strategy during and after the COVID-19 pandemic.

Higher Education Applications

The COVID-19 pandemic disrupted organizations and communities across the world. It certainly had a profound impact on the operations and finances of colleges and universities, and in many ways it helped to amplify the value of higher education as colleges and universities directly responded to the various needs imposed by the public health crisis. As explored in several sections of this book, the pandemic mobilized collective action, elevated critical research and community engagement efforts, and served as a catalyst for innovation and reinvention both inside and outside of the classroom setting. Despite this tremendous opportunity, the crisis led to widespread loss of life, increased financial pressures, and heightened feelings of isolation, burnout, and anxiety. This impact was not shared equally, however, as it manifested itself disproportionally based on racial, socioeconomic, and geographic disparities.

In the NYC Covid-19 Oral History, Narrative and Memory Project, a team of sociologists, oral historians, and anthropologists from Columbia University documented a more abstract crisis that went beyond the immediate and most obvious losses invoked by the pandemic—what was described as a "phenomenological model of crisis with no resolution." As a summary of the project in the *New York Times Magazine* notes, "Time basically stopped working" for the researchers involved (Mooallem & Gilbertson, 2023). Describing this situation in more detail, the summary distills the following: "People were stuck. With everything suddenly up for grabs—with people's identities undermined and their surroundings untrustworthy—the narrators struggled to negotiate, and find meaning in, the details of their daily lives. And without any sense of when the pandemic would end, it became impossible to break out of that malaise, to project oneself into a future that kept evaporating ahead of you." Unlike other crises that possess clearer boundaries around the points of commencement and conclusion, the pandemic extended across multiple years with phases of varying severity. As our collective understanding of the virus evolved, so too did the guidelines, norms, and practices associated with the response to this public health crisis. The Columbia sociologists who initiated the project, Ryan Hagen and Denise Milstein, are reported as using the term "ontological insecurity" to describe the sense of limbo associated with the pandemic, a play on Anthony Giddens's (1991) application of the concept of ontological security to sociology, which he describes as a "person's fundamental sense of safety in the world" (p. 38). If ontological security allows us "to keep a particular narrative going" (p. 54), it is the experience of ontological *in*security that threatens this narrative, violates one's sense of safety and security, and leads to a deficit of hope for a better tomorrow. The ontological insecurity associated with the COVID-19 pandemic and the relentless pressures in responding to a seemingly endless crisis triggered a collapse in sensemaking and demanded a leadership response to this breakdown.

One could turn to many different examples of pandemic-related leadership communication, including public speeches, press releases, organization-wide communiques, annual reports, and published strategic plans, goals, aspirations, and vision statements. These artifacts provide a glimpse into how leaders might stimulate meaning-making during a time of "unprecedented" disruption. If we examine the responses to the pandemic offered by university leaders across the Big Ten institutions, for example, we see a number of strategies deployed to frame the public health crisis and the role of the institution both now and in the future. These public statements characterized the pandemic as a profound, historic, and unprecedented disruption—a "grand challenge of our time"—with both an immediate and long-term impact. Some characterized the pandemic as a catalyst for innovation, an accelerant of significant trends, and a moment for deep reflection and a reconsideration of how and where we work. In addition to acknowledging the deeply rooted societal and structural issues that were further exposed by the pandemic, university leaders were also sure to frame the crisis as an invitation for a reset, as a once-in-a-lifetime opportunity to shape the future, and as a catalyst to invest in the restoration and growth of our institutions and communities. Finally, in attempting to derive meaning from the historic public health crisis, university leaders reconnected with the mission, purpose, and value proposition of institutions of higher education as beacons of hope, as frontline leaders in providing access to health care and research that could address the crisis, and as critical agents of change and transformation. As Fredrickson et al. (2003) suggest, "Finding positive meaning may be the most powerful leverage point for cultivating positive emotions during times of crisis" (p. 15), and this attempt to make sense of an otherwise senseless period of loss and uncertainty was evident in the messages put forward by university leaders during this time.

Other dominant themes represented in the public communication surrounding the pandemic by the Big Ten institutions include a focus on the successes accomplished in spite of the public health crisis and the various qualities embodied by the community in successfully responding to the pressures of the crisis, such as resilience, sacrifice, diligence, tireless efforts, endurance, stamina, dedication, spirit, resolve, nimbleness, and resourcefulness. These messages often articulated some vision for a more normal and stable future—one filled with hope, promise, and some degree of enthusiasm. Other dominant areas of focus include an emphasis on reimagining the ways in which work is accomplished in higher education and the experience one might be able to provide for current and future students. Reasserting a commitment to the common good, many of these messages acknowledged the institution's response in serving the community, state, nation, and world in the fight against COVID-19 and the various partnerships forged internally and externally in handling the crisis. Finally, in response to the widespread threat to individual and collective wellness, well-being, and safety, the public communication placed a prominent emphasis on the values of balance, humanity, compassion, kindness, responsiveness, empathy, and care.

In addition to these broader themes, a closer look at three institutions provides us with a glimpse into the unique framing strategies offered during this time of profound uncertainty.

In his first formal message as the new president of the University of Maryland in April 2021, Darryll J. Pines acknowledged a "time of remarkable disruption and uncertainty" amidst the "two pandemics" of COVID-19 and long-standing racial injustice. In response to the "grand challenges" of the moment, the new president invited the university community to "be bold" as he introduced some of his initial priorities for the institution. Announcing the launch of a formal strategic planning process, President Pines highlighted the charge to "re-imagine our campus and community as a modern flagship research university in the third decade of the 21st century." In a later message to the community in February 2022, he introduced the launch of an "ambitious" and "fearless" strategic plan titled "Fearlessly Forward: In Pursuit of Excellence and Impact for the Public Good: The University of Maryland Strategic Plan." In the midst of tremendous loss, unprecedented disruption, and an increasingly uncertain environment, the communication surrounding the strategic planning effort centered on "moving fearlessly forward to forge a better world for humankind."

At Rutgers University, another new president took the reins during the start of the COVID-19 pandemic. Sixteen months after taking office, President Jonathan Holloway was inaugurated as the twenty-first president of Rutgers, The State University of New Jersey. Referring to Rutgers as a "work in progress," Holloway used the metaphor of building a cathedral as a way to describe the ongoing care and commitment needed in tending to a community: "I believe in looking at the work before us as akin to the building of that metaphorical cathedral. I believe that as we go about our daily work we must always honor those who came before us, who also worked on this structure, and whose names may be lost to history. I believe that we must remain vigilant, aware that at any moment something can come along that could stress its walls, that could compromise its roof, or that could crack its foundation." From the start of his presidency, on July 1, 2020, Holloway was forced to respond to the enormous challenges of the dual pandemics. In his opening letter to the university community, Holloway indicated the following: "Soon after my January introduction as Rutgers' 21st president, the emergence of the COVID-19 pandemic made clear that the terms of my future presidency had changed. I don't need to tell anyone in New Jersey or at Rutgers how much damage COVID has caused personally, emotionally, psychologically, and financially. Because of these enormous setbacks, I will be focusing much of my initial energy as president on repair and rebuilding." In the pursuit of building a beloved community and with a commitment to honor and celebrate the excellence of the institution, Holloway engaged in—and continues to adopt—ideas and insights that encourage the repairing, rebuilding, and healing of an institution.

In one final example, we can direct our attention to the annual open letters issued by past president of Purdue University, Mitch Daniels. In his annual open letter to the "people of Purdue," Daniels (2021) provided updates on some of the more difficult decisions of his presidency in response to the COVID-19 pandemic. In reflecting on the challenges of 2020, Daniels offered the following:

> Someone has speculated that soon "2020" will enter our vernacular as a slang term for "miserable." In describing a business failure, a major sports beatdown, or just a really lousy day, maybe we'll say "It was a real 2020." That's one way to look at it. Another, as I have remarked to many of our students these last four months, is that 2020, at least at our university, can be remembered as a time of achievement, of adversity overcome through a genuine communal effort. In a time of depressing polarization and societal division, a community of 50,000 diverse citizens pulled together to do what so many said was not possible.

In the following year's open letter, Daniels (2022) titled one section "Leaving 2020 Behind," and elaborated on the ways one might describe Purdue as "a happy place," positioning the challenges associated with the public health crisis as history:

> "Happy" is, I believe, an apt word to describe the atmosphere on the West Lafayette campus these last few months. A couple of years back, a national journalist making his first visit to Purdue described it to his readers as "a happy place." I liked that at the time, reflecting on how many schools at which that adjective would not apply.
>
> But if the description was accurate then, I think it might have been even more so this fall. I checked my own impression with others many times until it became clear we all sensed the same thing: a palpable enthusiasm to be back together. It showed in attendance at events, including huge student sections at Ross-Ade and campus functions like Dance Marathon. But you could

simply tell it from the faces, especially of those freshmen who spent what should have been a great senior high school year locked down at home.

Despite their different framing strategies, metaphors, and underlying assumptions, these three examples offer a snapshot into how the presidents of selected Big Ten institutions chose to frame some of the complexities of the moment and the opportunities that might lie ahead. The decision to celebrate and honor the community for their response to the challenges of the moment, along with the strategy of reinforcing the cycles of learning and ethos of care that would help to move their institutions forward, can help others to find meaning and purpose when stability seems most at risk. Recall from earlier that sensemaking goes beyond interpretation and involves both authoring and creation—to bracket experiences in ways that are made sensible for others. As Seeger and Sellnow (2016) suggest, "Memories of a crisis tend to become homogenized over time, and the collective memory of an event becomes a universal and generalized meaning. In some cases, the collective meaning becomes almost mythic and may take on the status of a metanarrative" (p. 38). As we continue to move beyond the immediate risks of COVID-19 and as the immediate memories of this crisis and other related crises of the moment fade from view, the post-crisis efforts by leaders to help stimulate meaning-making may help to constitute and inform the metanarratives that will ultimately serve as a guide for sensemaking in response to future moments of exigency.

Considerations for Post-Crisis Leadership Action

Efforts to stimulate meaning-making in the aftermath of crisis require calm and composed leadership, along with the ability to engage in meaningful communication with individuals who are experiencing heightened emotions. In addition to the many applied recommendations described by the authors cited in this chapter on sensemaking, framing, and the management of meaning, those seeking to engage in this important work in the aftermath of crisis may find these additional considerations to be of value:

- Know your audience. This fundamental principle for effective communication becomes especially important when attempting to find common ground and meaningfully connect with those most directly involved with a crisis.
- Communication is consequential (Pearce & Cronen, 1980). Communicate and behave with intentionality and purpose, recognizing that words and actions communicate intended and unintended messages with multiple possibilities for interpretation and misinterpretation (Ruben & Gigliotti, 2016).
- Identify and connect with the values, norms, and principles of mutual interest for you and the members of your unit, department, or institution. As Seeger and Sellnow (2016) note, "Meaning making is a complex psychological process that incorporates the construction of global, fundamental, and relatively stable beliefs, assumptions, and expectations about the world" (p. 38). When the conditions of the moment are characterized by fear, panic, or uncertainty, these enduring and shared values or principles can help to bring comfort and community during a time when it is most needed.
- Crises disrupt existing meaning systems, and leaders serve an important role in helping to provide potential explanations for the disruption in ways that require trust. By speaking honestly, sticking to the facts of the situation, avoiding rumors, and indicating when they might not know the answer, leaders can build rapport and trust with those dealing with the aftermath of a crisis.
- The co-construction of meaning relies less on knowing all answers and more on posing questions and possibilities that allow for a shared construction of the situation.
- Invoke hope and optimism in ways that invite individuals to find some sense of meaning in response to tragedy.
- Listen with sincerity, grace, and a willingness to learn.

- Recognize the distinct ways in which individuals will personally move through the sensemaking process and acknowledge that there is no one shared timeline that governs this process.
- Encourage storytelling and reflection in response to trauma. As suggested by the School Crisis Recovery & Renewal Project (n.d.), "Crisis leaders need to understand the physical and psychological disruptions that are a common consequence of trauma. Trauma interrupts our ability to maintain a coherent narrative that explains our world and our place within it. We as humans need a worldview of ourselves and each other that makes sense to us. This sense-making narrative helps us interpret the past, negotiate the present, and move comfortably into the future. One of the functions of a crisis is that it interrupts our regular story: trauma can pause our bodies and brains at the moment of harm. We need crisis leaders to help us create meaning from our trauma experiences, which then helps our bodies and brains integrate the crisis into our larger story. Storytelling and reflection are essential to our collective crisis healing."
- In an attempt to make and find meaning from loss, Walsh (2007) notes that "it is important to contextualize . . . distress as understandable and common among those who have experienced similar tragedies" (p. 211).

As these practices seem to suggest, the work of meaning-making is an inherently relational endeavor. Understandably, the pressures of the moment often place many demands on those engaged in leadership, and these crisis situations initially possess a great deal of uncertainty. In moving from the crisis to post-crisis phase, more details will likely come into focus regarding the cause and impact of the critical incident, and with this increased clarity also emerges a window of opportunity for the co-construction of meaning. Additionally, in this shift from crisis to post-crisis, one might also encounter increased calls for reinvention, which is the primary focus of chapter 4.

4

Pursue Reinvention

There is no shortage of challenges and pressures facing institutions of higher education, including those posed by decreasing enrollments, diminishing state funding, troubling completion rates, declining world rankings, mounting concerns regarding student debt, growing politicized attacks on diversity and inclusion efforts, and the expanding consideration of more affordable, direct-to-career alternatives to a four-year degree. According to a survey of higher education leaders conducted by the Association of Public and Land-Grant Universities (2020) in partnership with Blue Moon Consulting Group and SimpsonScarborough, the challenges facing the sector have been exacerbated as a result of the pandemic, with government funding, student mental health, and diversity and inclusion recognized as most significant. Writing for *Forbes*, Rosowsky (2020) noted that "the pandemic hit at a time when higher education already was facing tremendous financial, demographic, and public perception challenges. There were growing questions about value, return-on-investment, relevance, and need."

Despite the list of widespread challenges and pressures that may at times seem paralyzing to institutions and their leaders, there remain tremendous opportunities for colleges and universities to explore strategies for reinvention—or what might otherwise be described as transformation, reimagination, and revitalization. For example, the evolution of online education, industry and community partnerships, artificial intelligence, competency-based education, and alternative credentials present colleges and universities with many potential avenues for growth and innovation. As suggested by Gregory Fowler, president of the University of Maryland Global Campus, "I think a big part of the future of higher education is seeing it less as a one-stop shop where you can come and get your degree and more of a place where you can get the experience you need when you need it, and when you need to go back, you know where to go" (McKenzie, 2021). This sentiment reflects the spirit of the 60-Year Curriculum initiative at Harvard University, the lifetime education model at Georgia Tech University, and the emergence of what Michael Crow and William Dabars at Arizona State University characterize as the New American University that can accelerate social change through broad access to world-class knowledge production and cutting-edge technological innovation. In a 2021 survey of college presidents conducted by *Inside Higher Ed*, 58 percent of responding presidents strongly agreed that the COVID-19 pandemic shifted the mindset on campus toward transformation, and 52 percent noted that some pandemic-related changes would stick, including increased online learning options (83%), additional flexibility for staff to work remotely (76%), additional investments in mental health services (75%), and more stackable certificates and other alternatives to existing degrees (50%).

The act of reinvention allows for individual and collective transformation in both appearance and/or function. As some definitions highlight, reinvention involves changing "something so much that it appears to be entirely new" (Oxford University Press, n.d.) or "the act of producing something new based on something that already exists, or the new thing that is produced" (Cambridge University and Assessment, n.d.). Reinvention allows one to exercise some degree of influence in shaping the future, to turn to the next chapter, to create something new out of that which already exists. In a quote attributed to the German painter and sculptor Anselm Kiefer, "Ruins, for me, are the beginning. With the debris, you can construct new ideas." Reinvention can be incremental or transformational, and efforts to replace the old with the new can be generated from the bottom up or may be imposed from above. Reinvention involves change, and, as is well documented in the change literature, resistance to change is inevitable among individuals, groups, and organizations. In much the same way as this resistance can be viewed as a liability or opportunity, so too can efforts at reinvention threaten the status quo or invite fresh and inspiring possibilities for the future.

Crises create windows of opportunity for pursuing reinvention. In some cases, as a "necessary corrective," the crisis helps to reveal a deficiency, blind spot, upstream factor, or root issue in need of attention. In other cases, the crisis brings people together in ways that are otherwise atypical and allows for the emergence of alternative paradigms—new ways of viewing the purpose, goals, or strategy of the organization. As suggested by the literature on chaos theory, "Crisis is a necessary part of organizing in that it helps the system purge outdated elements creating opportunities for new growth. Points of bifurcation allow the system to radically change direction, character, or structure and create a new, sometimes entirely unexpected order" (Murphy, 1996, as cited in Seeger & Ulmer, 2002, p. 137). For many organizations, particularly those rooted in deep and historic traditions, the crisis can serve as a catalyst for change that might otherwise be considered unnecessary or unimportant during periods of stability. This chapter will take a closer look at the promise and pitfalls of reinvention, focusing on post-crisis leadership strategies that can help the organization to move forward with purpose and clarity, along with the risks that come into play if these efforts are perceived by others to be hurried, unnecessary, or problematic.

The Promise and Pitfalls of Reinvention

There are many pundits and commentators advocating for the reinvention of higher education. A sentiment that was commonly discussed and the source of widespread debate prior to the pandemic, calls for reinventing higher education grew in frequency and popularity as colleges and universities responded to the health crisis, and this tension regarding the need for widespread reinvention lingers today. Here is a snapshot of some of the calls to rebuild, reform, and reinvent higher education published within various news outlets:

- "We're in the process of reinvention, whether we like it or not. Post-COVID will not look like pre-COVID" (Llopis, 2020).
- "We are at the confluence of massive economic, technologic, and social changes that demand higher education do more than small fixes. We will not thrive if we merely tweak the system to replicate practices of the lecture hall in an online delivery system" (Schroeder, 2021).
- "The redesign of our higher education system needs to take place now, or we risk slowing the tide of America's recovery from the COVID-19 crisis" (Jindal, 2021).
- "How do we make the most of this crisis? We have the opportunity to rebuild a more flexible, consumer-centric, higher education system, one that is more responsive to the needs of students and employers alike, and offers greater flexibility, quality, and relevance" (Hu & Ton-Quinlivan, 2021).
- "COVID-19 is a crisis of terrifying proportions; the struggle ahead is over how we respond to it. Given America's history, this response will be shaped, to a large degree, by the persistence of structural racism, on the one hand, and our commitment to racial justice, on the other. We can seize this moment and remake the university into something that is inclusive and liberating, or reinforce long-standing and destructive inequities. If we choose the former path, everyone will benefit" (Taylor, 2020).

Writing for the *Chronicle of Higher Education*, Paquette (2021) questions the degree to which "higher education can save itself" and points to the flourishing "cottage industry of diagnosis, prognostication, and reinvention." The author goes on to state:

> Pundits diverge, however, on the strategies and tactics needed [to save higher education]. They fall into three broad categories. First, there are defenders of the status quo, who assert the fundamental solidity of the existing order and the wisdom of keeping calm and carrying on. Second, there are utopians—self-appointed guardians of long-cherished values—who gaze nostalgically back to a lost golden age or await some exogenous panacea. Third, there are reformers: proponents of pragmatic yet sometimes sweeping change. This final group is subdivided between those who focus on the microdynamics of curricula and program design and those who seek to recast higher education's role in society writ large.

The debate surrounding reinvention often focuses on competing views of higher education as a private good or public good. The paradigm of neoliberalism and the assumptions and public policies that reflect this view tend to focus on efficiency, market competition, and college education as a financial investment for the student and a mechanism for serving the needs and demands of the business community (Mintz, 2021; Saltmarsh, 2011). As a public good, however, advocates turn to issues of social mobility, access, responsibility to the tax-paying public, and a wide range of public benefits derived from the tripartite mission of teaching, research, and service that guide institutions of higher education (Howard, 2014).

Calls for reinvention often take their cue from the troubling trend lines, projections, and sources of data that paint a picture of an industry in distress. Continued declines in year-to-year enrollment, what Alexander (2013, 2018) hypothesizes as "peak higher education," along with declining birth rates, fewer international and immigrant students, and growing competition present a challenging backdrop for colleges and universities. In his provocatively titled article, "Here's How Higher Education Dies," Harris (2018) writes about how many institutions will be shielded from the pattern of declining enrollment, but in the spirit of reinvention, "most colleges will not be so fortunate. They will either have to adapt or die out."

But are predictions regarding the existential threat to colleges and universities overstated? In response to claims insisting on the demise of American universities, Brint (2019) declares a "golden age of research" and calls attention to the positive trends regarding research expenditures at major research universities, research publications, and labor-saving technologies that allow for enhanced research productivity. The enduring purpose of higher education, the mission of teaching, research, and service—and in some cases, community engagement and/or clinical excellence—elevates the work of higher education, and despite the intersecting challenges that threaten the work of the academy, colleges and universities continue to supply three essential ingredients that contribute to national progress, according to Derek Bok (2013), a former president of Harvard University. These include "new discoveries in science, technology, and other fields of inquiry; expert knowledge of the kind essential to the work of most important institutions; and well-trained adults with the skills required to practice the professions, manage a wide variety of organizations, and perform an increasing proportion of the more demanding jobs in an advanced, technologically sophisticated economy (p. 1). Nannerl Keohane (2006), a former president of Wellesley College and Duke University, highlights the "moral purpose" of colleges and universities and their critical role in "determining whether humanity will indeed have a future, and what it will be like." For some, reinvention may impede the pursuit of this moral purpose, whereas others may see it as our only hope of achieving this purpose within an increasingly complicated and competitive ecosystem.

Although the death throes of higher education have been greatly exaggerated, the sector as a whole faces an array of challenges that require strategic attention. Many of these challenges—accelerated due to the converging crises of this recent period—threaten the long-term viability of many colleges and universities and make critical the goal of reinvention, transformation, or reimagination. As we take a closer look at the experience of those engaged in leadership "on the ground" in higher education—academic department chairs—these competing views of reinvention come into focus.

Competing Views of Post-Crisis Reinvention

In normal circumstances, the role of the academic department chair is both complex and ambiguous—often caught between diverging interests of faculty and administration (Bowman, 2002; Buller, 2012; Chu, 2012; Gmelch & Miskin, 2004; Gmelch & Parkay, 1999). During the early days of the pandemic in the United States, it was clear from conversations with individuals at my institution and others that these highly complicated academic leadership roles had become especially overwhelming. Drawing upon a sample of nearly eight hundred department chairs from the Big Ten, a survey was sent to this population during April and May 2020, followed by another survey in August 2021. Respondents to the first survey included 172 department leaders representing all but one of the Big Ten universities, followed by 115 respondents from all Big Ten institutions to the second survey. As reported in Gigliotti (2021, 2022b), the findings from the first wave of survey responses point to intensified leadership challenges for chairs and the need to pivot extensively in addressing the unique and urgent needs of administrators, faculty and staff colleagues, and students. As one chair described the burden of responsibility in the first survey, "I feel as though I now operate a 1–800 hotline answering questions all day long given the uncertainty people have about classes, teaching, research, grants, payroll, etc. It is truly exhausting." These findings echo many of the responses shared in the second wave of the study, with an added emphasis on feelings of burnout, stress, and exhaustion in the responses to the August 2021 survey. As one chair noted, "Honestly, I feel jaded and exhausted. I just hope I can muster the energy to struggle through this year."

Situated at the nexus of faculty, administration, and students, department chairs are engaged in critical work for institutions of higher education, with some characterizing these roles as most influential given their proximity and ability to connect with students, faculty, and staff in ways that more senior administrators might find more difficult (Hlavac & Buller, 2020). As calls for "reinventing higher education" grow in number and intensity in response to existing crises, department chairs serving on the front lines of academic leadership are likely to play an important role in reinvention efforts. For some, their role will be as agents of influence in leading the reinvention of policies, practices, and patterns of behavior at the departmental level and throughout their academic discipline. Others may resist such calls out of fear, disregard, or distrust of the financial and existential crises posed by reinvention efforts.

When asked in April and May 2020 to assess current views of the post-crisis reinvention of higher education on a scale of 1 (strongly negative) to 5 (strongly positive), the results were divided, with 19 respondents (24%) viewing reinvention as either extremely or somewhat negative, 31 respondents (38%) viewing reinvention as either extremely or somewhat positive, and 31 (38%) respondents indicating neither a positive nor negative view. The responses in August 2021 were slightly less positive, with 35 respondents (36%) indicating an extremely or somewhat negative view of reinvention, 26 respondents (28%) indicating an extremely or somewhat positive view, and 35 respondents (36%) suggesting neither a positive nor negative perspective.

When respondents were asked to elaborate on their perceptions of reinvention, the responses offered during both points in time provide a glimpse into the challenges associated with post-crisis leadership. For some, the pursuit of reinvention is seen as an opportunity for needed change and a catalyst to help move an organization forward, whereas others offer a more cynical perspective that makes the work of post-crisis reinvention in higher education potentially fraught with tension. For those who expressed a more favorable view of reinvention, respondents described the opportunities for innovation, creativity, and growth that have been made possible due to the impact of the pandemic. Describing "necessity as the mother of invention," one chairperson indicated the ways in which the pandemic "forced us into innovative models that otherwise would have taken years to implement." As another chair noted, "Much of what is best about traditional higher education will still be valued, while at the same time, this unexpected circumstance is causing us to have new and innovative discussions." A number of chairs reflected on the growing recognition of the value of online education and remote instruction, while also commenting on the "lack of in-person interactions [as] detrimental to the education of our students." For some, the notion of crisis as a necessary corrective led them to posit a favorable view of reinvention. For example, according to one chairperson, "Higher education was in crisis before the pandemic. There are a lot of things we need to fix. Massive state underfunding, administrative bloat, obscene salaries paid to athletics, reliance on cheap contingent labor, and graduate programs which are training students for a market that really does not exist anymore. The pandemic has laid bare all sorts of inequalities, so we need to do some fundamental fixing. I am not sure we can, but I think the discussions are useful."

The slow-moving and deliberative traditions of higher education have been called into question, and of the department chairs who reviewed reinvention in a favorable light, several acknowledged the ability to respond in a more agile and purposeful way to the challenges of the academy. As one individual noted, "Higher education 'suffers' from a large amount of inertia. Crises make us take stock and re-evaluate priorities. If a better understanding of priorities results from this crisis, and if we resolve to actively work toward satisfying the most important priorities, the resultant changes will end up being somewhat positive." Recognizing the double-edged impact, another chair invoked the imagery of the punctuated equilibrium theory of evolution: "There are times or events that turn the world on its head after periods of relative calm. The calm periods lead to small incremental changes in the way we do business, but it is the catastrophic events that lead to rapid innovation. Unfortunately, those periods are ones in which there is loss, and I believe that we will see a great deal of 'radiation' in higher ed, but also a lot of 'extinction.'"

This idea of extinction, along with the many threats posed by the pandemic, led many department chairs to critique views of reinvention. As one chair noted, "I did not think it needed reinvention. This seems like a b-school [business school] term for consultants." Another individual described reinvention as a threat to liberal education: "The last decade of funding cuts have left public higher education fiscally exposed to such a crisis. The reinvention will be driven by fiscal concerns and not pedagogical or intellectual interests, and is sure to have more negative consequences than benefits. This crisis will provide a strong push further down the dubious path towards a mission of workforce development rather than a broad liberal education." Reflecting on the financial impact of the crisis, one chair commented on the ways in which "budgets at public universities will likely be drastically affected by the economic disruption associated with the pandemic for years to come. My concern is that the 'reinvention' may amount to being asked to do more with less: fewer full-time faculty, more deferred maintenance, smaller investments in infrastructure, etc." A negative view of reinvention seemed to align with a negative outlook on the state of affairs in general. As one respondent described, "Right now there is too much of a state of disarray to feel positive about the future direction in which we are headed."

The shift to a fully online teaching, learning, and working environment led many respondents to view reinvention in a more negative light. According to one, "Online education falls well short of the quality education to which our students are accustomed." Or, as another department chair commented, "I am not opposed to some increase in the amount of remote teaching we do. But I think it is less than ideal, and I fear that this crisis will enable universities to increase remote teaching in ways that outstrip its pedagogical usefulness." The sudden shift to a fully remote context led several chairs to question the value of making larger structural changes without considering the short- and long-term impact of such decisions. For instance, one chair offered this poignant observation: "The solution of online teaching can only be accepted at this time of emergency, and it is already presenting so many problems, from logistical issues to psychological concerns, let alone pedagogical difficulties. Given the predicted duration of the contagion, the [persistence of online teaching] may be a necessity, but it is certainly, in my view, a negative necessity, especially if it will encourage the academic world to support that technological path and downsize the conventional forms of teaching, with the risk of reducing the number of faculty members."

Finally, of the respondents who provided a neutral rating of their view of the post-crisis reinvention of higher education, many reflected on the ambiguity and subjectivity of reinvention. For example, as one department chair shared, "I have no idea at this point what on earth that will mean. If it means the further hollowing out of public investment in education, then reinvention will mean disaster. If it means that we can realize the importance of the university to the vibrancy of our country, and reinvest, then I think we might be able to reinvent in very important ways. But the temporary movement of instruction to remote models is not a reinvention. Don't be silly." Or, in highlighting the dual views of reinvention, one chair described the tension as follows:

> I don't know what to think of this. I think some who have long advocated for IMPROVING the quality of teaching and learning experiences are calling for using this pandemic as a timely opportunity to push all of us to more effectively orient ourselves to what we SHOULD have been doing all along (e.g., more active learning, experiential learning, greater use of

backward design, flipped classrooms, greater intentionality, etc.). But, I also think some (particularly those who have been railing against the commercialization, corporatization, or neoliberalizing of higher education) think of the "reinvention" of higher education in a very different way. And their cynical take on this "reinvention" is a warning to us all to not allow these above economic trends to take further hold in our educational institution.

Finally, as many chairs commented, "it is too early to tell" and "there are currently far too many unknowns, recognizing that perspectives on reinvention will continue to evolve as institutions of higher education come to terms with the short- and long-term impact of the pandemic."

Revisiting Institutional Strategy in Higher Education

The pursuit of reinvention in the aftermath of crisis may lead to a shift in institutional strategy, and it is useful to consider how the writing on organizational strategy might intersect with calls for organizational transformation post-crisis. An organization's strategy extends beyond the words and goals articulated in any formal plan. For example, we might turn to Mintzberg's (1987) five definitions of strategy in considering the various components of institutional strategy that may undergo some degree of transformation or reinvention:

- *Strategy as plan*—"some sort of *consciously intended* course of action, a guideline (or set of guidelines) to deal with a situation"
- *Strategy as pattern*—"a pattern in a stream of actions" that focuses on the resulting behavior of the plan"
- *Strategy as ploy*—focused on the "what" of strategy, including the source for which resources are deployed and for what purposes
- *Strategy as position*—"a means of locating an organization" in the external environment

- *Strategy as perspective*—"its content consisting not just of a chosen position, but of an ingrained way of perceiving the world" (pp. 11–16)

In describing a "good strategy," Rumelt (2011) notes the following: "Good strategy has an essential logical structure that I call the kernel. The kernel of a strategy contains three elements: a diagnosis, a guiding policy, and coherent action. The guiding policy specifies the approach to dealing with the obstacles called out in the diagnosis. It is like a signpost, marking the direction forward but not defining the details of the trip. Coherent actions are feasible coordinated policies, resource commitments, and actions designed to carry out the guiding policy" (p. 16). He highlights four signs of a flawed strategy: (1) fluff, (2) failure to face the problem, (3) mistaking goals for strategy, and (4) fuzzy or overly complex strategic objectives. According to Rumelt, "To obtain higher performance, leaders must identify the critical obstacles to forward progress and then develop a coherent approach to overcoming them" (p. 51). This intersection with leadership extends into Kaplan and Norton's (2001) work on strategy-focused organizations, involving five central steps:

1. Translate the strategy into operational terms.
2. Align the organization to the strategy.
3. Make strategy everyone's everyday job.
4. Make strategy a continual process.
5. Mobilize change through executive leadership. (p. 9)

Much of the writing on strategy tends to focus upon corporate applications. Approaches to setting and pursuing strategy in higher education require an adaptation to the unique mission(s), vocabulary, culture, and engagement practices found within institutions of higher education (Ruben et al., 2021). Effective strategy in an academic context can specify directions that are meaningful and mobilizing for faculty, staff, students, and other key stakeholders in higher education. Furthermore, an inclusive approach to designing, planning, and implementing strategy can promote ownership of and a commitment to the strategy and its realization (Tromp & Ruben, 2021).

Writing specifically about strategic planning in an academic environment, Keller (1983) highlighted the importance of considering questions such as "What business are we really in?," "What is most central to us?," and "How shall we proceed?" (p. 72). Unlike other forms of planning, strategic planning focuses on determining and guiding outcomes rather than falling victim to the myriad external forces that routinely bombard organizations. Writing for the *Review of Higher Education*, Hardy et al. (1983) describe how "the conventional view of strategy—as a plan, or a set of explicit intentions preceding and controlling actions—is too narrow to permit a satisfactory understanding of strategy formulation in the university setting" (p. 407). The authors go on to acknowledge four general propositions that remain true four decades later:

1. Many different actors are involved in the strategy formation process in universities.
2. Some of the university's strategies pertain to the whole, others to particular parts.
3. We should expect to find a good deal of fragmentation in the strategies pursued by universities.
4. Control of specific strategies may reside with individual professors, within the administrative structure, or in the collectivity. (pp. 423–424)

The unique structure, governance, and decision-making patterns found in higher education complicate the work of strategy design and formulation in this context; yet as the earlier discussion of challenges and opportunities makes clear, there is tremendous value in aligning efforts across the institution in a shared direction in order to weather collective challenges, ensure consistency of strategy, and reimagine the work of the academy in response to the current environment. Furthermore, as supported by the literature and the experiences of anyone who has engaged in this work in higher education, the meaningful, systematic, and inclusive engagement of others is critical to the success of setting and pursuing strategy in this context—and this holds true during the post-crisis period. If strategy provides a guide for who we are, who we want to be, and who we are not—questions that are constitutive of and deeply wrapped up in one's core identity—calls to shift strategic direction under the auspices of reinvention are likely to encounter some degree of resistance.

Resistance to Reinvention

Change does not occur in a vacuum. Rather, as Buller (2014) notes, if one is going to lead change effectively, one must understand the system in which the change will occur. Despite being a constant in organizations of all kinds, change can be a profoundly uncomfortable experience for many, and one can expect to encounter some degree of resistance to change in any system. Crises can serve as catalysts for change; yet in attempting to pursue reinvention or pivot in new strategic directions as an organization in the aftermath of the crisis, those engaged in leadership may encounter resistance. In *Whatever It Is, I'm Against It: Resistance to Change in Higher Education*, Brian Rosenberg (2023), president emeritus of Macalester College and visiting professor in the Harvard Graduate School of Education, summarizes the key theme of the book: "The resistance to anything like serious change is profound. By 'change' I don't mean the addition of yet another program or the alteration of a graduation requirement, but something that is transformational and affects the way we do our work on a deep level" (para. 8). This resistance may take the form of avoidance, questioning, challenging, delaying, withdrawing, and even sabotaging the planned change (Ruben et al., 2021). It is often due, in part, to a general cynicism associated with any organizational change; feelings of fatigue associated with the scale and pace of change efforts;

disagreement with the proposed change or process for instituting the change; or an excess of change priorities and messages that can spread confusion or disengagement across a team, organization, or community. As indicated by some of the department chairs' reactions to reinvention above, some may view such a change as unnecessary, unproductive, or, in some cases, as a threat to what is believed to be an essential purpose of higher education. Similar to designing and executing planned change initiatives during times of organizational stability, leading change in the aftermath of crisis requires a commitment to engagement, input solicitation, and securing coalitions of support—and this is especially important given the commitment to shared governance in higher education.

Similar to leading change during noncrisis periods, resistance can stall change and reinvention efforts. As noted by Lawrence (1969), "When resistance does appear, it should not be thought of as something to be overcome. Instead, it can best be thought of as a useful red flag—a signal that something is going wrong. To use a rough analogy, signs of resistance in a social organization are useful in the same way that pain is useful to the body as a signal that some bodily functions are getting out of adjustment." Lewis and Russ (2012) extend this further in describing the ways in which "input solicitation during change might also yield important critiques of change and that surfacing such criticisms might actually improve change efforts and/or help organizations reconsider whether the change is as beneficial as originally thought by decision makers" (p. 272). Rather than interpreting resistance as a barrier to leading change, an alternative view allows us to see resistance as a useful and important dimension of successful change efforts—and this is perhaps even more relevant when attempting to lead a group of people or an organization through change after experiencing some degree of loss, disruption, or trauma.

If the pursuit of reinvention or a new strategic direction remains a goal in the aftermath of crisis, one should anticipate resistance and take action to mitigate change cynicism and fatigue, build trust among individuals or groups most impacted by the change, seek out and truly consider feedback from others with a willingness to modify the change, involve others in the implementation process, and stay focused on the process through which new changes are implemented. Importantly, by soliciting the input of others along the way, those engaged in leadership can develop a deeper understanding of the source(s) of resistance and take the necessary steps to address this resistance in pursuing a change. Or, through ongoing dialogue, one may reconsider the change or approach it in different ways that are informed by the feedback of others.

The following framework developed by Ruben (2011) serves as a useful reference for leading change. Although not designed specifically for post-crisis reinvention efforts, the steps outlined in the model provide a guide for how one might approach change in the aftermath of crisis. As the fog of crisis settles, one might move through these steps in a somewhat accelerated way depending on the scope of the crisis and the urgency of the need for change.

1. *Attention*—capture attention in a world of many people and ideas competing for your time. This step requires you to emphasize the need for change and generate a sense of importance and urgency for the change. As part of this effort, you might also create a "burning platform," a process that helps others to understand the consequences of not changing, by highlighting the reasons why the status quo may lead to undesirable outcomes in the future.

2. *Engagement*—involve appropriate individuals and constituencies in a discussion of the challenges/problems and solutions. The primary goal at this point in the process is facilitating dialogue with internal and external stakeholders—including individuals who may support or resist the change—in order to generate a shared understanding of the reasons for the proposed change, what the change will involve, and how it will be an improvement over the current situation (see also Gigliotti et al., 2017).

3. *Resolve*—developing resolve, which involves promoting a commitment to the advocated change, is the third step of the

change process. This stage is focused on building coalitions of support for the change, which requires a candid and honest discussion of areas of agreement and potential obstacles. At this point in the process, developing resolve and commitment will also necessitate a focus on the needed resources to move the change forward and provide abundant opportunities for input and idea generation among the members of the team, group, organization, or community.

4. *Action*—the fourth step in this model is the call to action. As you might suspect, this tends to be where most change leadership efforts begin—to recognize the need for change and to take necessary actions in addressing the change. However, successful change is often the result of careful attention to the process through which you consider diverse perspectives and build a coalition of support on behalf of the change. Thus, motivating action builds on successful efforts in each of the prior steps. The stages involved in this step include clarifying intended change outcomes, promoting the desired behavior, identifying the tasks or actions that need to be implemented, providing the necessary resources and training to support the desired behaviors, prompting activities that move the initiative in the desired direction, and continuing these efforts until the intended change outcomes are realized (see also Gigliotti et al., 2017).

5. *Integration*—the final step is focused on integrating and institutionalizing the change into the culture of the group, organization, or community. If you think about any personal changes you have attempted to engage in over the years—learning a new skill, stopping a bad habit, or developing a new routine—sustaining the change is often a source of great challenge. In order to assure integration, you might consider pursuing strategies for celebrating the change, developing mechanisms to reinforce the change, implementing strategies to allow for the continuous review and refinement of the change, and cultivating a network of support upon which you and others can lean in pursuing the change over time.

Ultimately, the success of any change effort, including efforts to engage in organizational reinvention in the aftermath of crisis, hinges on the presence of trust, goodwill, and a recognition of the perceived value of the reinvention. Moving systematically through the framework noted above will not guarantee the success of a planned change, of course, but the goal is to adopt greater intentionality regarding your approach to leading organizational reinvention. A deficit of trust in leadership can jeopardize the success of any reinvention effort, stall attempts for reform, or discredit new strategic directions that are introduced in the post-crisis period. Furthermore, as will be explored in chapter 5, tensions may arise post-crisis regarding whether to bounce back to what once was or to look ahead to what might have never been. Leadership words, actions, and ways of being play a critical role in navigating these co-existing sources of tension.

Considerations for Post-Crisis Leadership Action

The convergence of recent challenges has exposed institutional liabilities, accelerated the need for change, and highlighted the value of innovative university endeavors in responding to an array of institutional and environmental setbacks. At the same time, these challenges—accompanied by myriad future opportunities—have reinforced the need to pursue a coherent and ambitious strategy with zeal and intentionality. As Selingo (2022) notes, "The challenge for colleges as they plan for this postpandemic future is to pay greater attention to real differentiation in the market instead of staking their future on tweaking the edges of what they're already doing" (p. 3). For some institutions, reinvention may involve a name change, the transition from an R2 to R1 Carnegie Research Classification, a new marketing campaign, or the development of a new global campus focused on expanding online degree programs—all of which we've seen take shape in this postpandemic environment. Other areas for reinvention are noted in table 4 and touch upon various sources of potential innovation.

TABLE 4 Opportunity Mapping: Five Key Areas Where Institutions Can Innovate on Their Models to Compete in the Decade Ahead

	FROM	TO
Digital backbone	Schools and departments siloed from each other	A real-time data stream that provides cross-institutional insight about students, talent, and financial position
Student experience	Process-centered approach where services are spread across campus and full of friction for the student	A seamless, interconnected experience that enables frequent interactions with students
Learner segmentation	Picture students mostly through the lens of age: traditional (18 to 22 years old) and non-traditional (everyone else)	Using student data and survey research, segment learners based on their motivation and mindset and build new offerings and services for them
Value equation	Touting economic benefits of going to college by riding the coattails of national averages	A quality and relevant learning experience that has a bearing on success and well-being in life
Partnerships	Sharing of back-office operations	Coalitions that include private partners to solve a common set of problems among institutions

SOURCE: Adapted from Selingo (2022, p. 10).

As leaders navigate the complexities of transformation in the aftermath of crisis, the following considerations for post-crisis reinvention may serve as a guide:

- Engage in the co-construction of reinvention efforts that draw upon the input, feedback, and buy-in of members of the community.
- Develop a cadence for the reinvention effort that meets the moment, taking account of the impact of the crisis on the emotional state of various stakeholders, the waves of change that may have preceded the crisis, and the history with organizational change

and transformation that might influence how new strategic directions are perceived by others.

- Recall that organizational reinvention does not have to be radical. Drawing upon some of the definitions introduced at the outset of this chapter, the act of reinvention allows for individual and collective transformation in both appearance and/or function, and even minor changes or improvements in the work of the organization can energize a community post-crisis.
- The reinvention of processes, systems, structures, and organizational identities must not lose sight of the individuals who are impacted by these planned changes. Although resistance is likely to be present, tap into this resistance as a source of learning and feedback to inform the reinvention effort.

This focus on reinvention remains a topic of widespread interest across higher education, particularly in response to declining confidence in higher education itself (Brenan, 2023). As M. D. Smith (2023) highlights, "Americans are waking up to the fact that our system of higher education is broken." The author goes on to describe examples of institutions who are leaning into this "once-in-a-lifetime opportunity to create a more open, flexible, inclusive, and lower-priced system that can scale to accommodate the hundreds of thousands of capable students who are being left behind." We must remain attentive to how this storyline unfolds and the ways in which these reinvention efforts might propel institutions forward—and to the setbacks that might result from such efforts. Reinvention in the aftermath of crisis will look different for each institution, and as we collectively look ahead to what might lie beyond the crisis, seizing opportunities for reinvention, reimagination, and transformation in ways that resonate with the campus community can help an organization to move forward. Ultimately, as described in chapter 5, such efforts can also help the organization to heal.

5

Advance Renewal

Internal and external stakeholders impacted by crises crave hope, compassion, and trust—and engaging these audiences in co-creating a path forward can cultivate resilience and renewal, focusing on both a return to what was and a pivot to what might have never been, as we saw in chapter 4. To illustrate the possibilities for healing that lie in the aftermath of crisis, we can turn our attention to incidents in 2020 and 2021 that triggered a racial reckoning in the United States. On May 25, 2020, Minneapolis police officers arrested George Floyd, a forty-six-year-old Black man, after a convenience store employee called 911 and told the police that Floyd had bought cigarettes with a counterfeit $20 bill. Floyd was handcuffed and pinned down by three white police officers. One of the officers pressed his knee on Floyd's neck for nearly nine and a half minutes, with Floyd pleading he could not breathe. A video of his death was captured by a bystander and led to protests across the globe and a collective reckoning around issues of racism, racial justice, and policing in the United States.

The tragic death of Floyd, along with the killings by police of other Black Americans in recent years, fueled a demand for truth, reconciliation, and redress for historical racial injustices. The social unrest and activism of 2020 pushed colleges and universities to acknowledge the history of their entanglements with various forms of white supremacy—especially slavery (Baldwin, 2021).

As Baldwin (2021) notes, "Delving deeper into the archive of higher education's racial history demands a reckoning that reaches far beyond slavery. This is a history that stretches from human bondage and land seizures to residential segregation and neighborhood demolitions, with a legacy of inheritance that certainly touches our present."

The post-crisis leadership practice featured in this chapter—advancing renewal—speaks to the importance of adopting people-centered leadership in the aftermath of trauma. The work of renewal involves an intentional commitment to acknowledge painful realities, privilege an ethic of care, and engage in meaningful dialogue in order to co-construct a desirable future state. As detailed further in this chapter, the response by colleges and universities to this national racial reckoning provides a glimpse into the dynamics of post-crisis renewal.

The scenes and sounds of crisis—such as in the death of Floyd—leave a lasting imprint on members of a community. Crises often strike at the core of an organization, violating the mission, disrupting normal operations, and destabilizing what may come to be expected as a normal and predictable source of order for internal beneficiaries and constituencies. Certainly, these experiences can influence the way an organization is depicted by the media and the ways in which it might be viewed by others, which can have a detrimental impact on various metrics viewed as most critical for an institution's sustainability and long-term success in an increasingly competitive landscape. Beyond the reputational, operational, and financial impact of such incidents, these critical moments directly and indirectly impact human lives. Many events and situations that are characterized as crises often threaten one's sense of well-being, and in the most devastating of cases, result in the loss of human life. In such circumstances, the post-crisis leadership imperative is centered on the renewal and healing of those affected by the crisis. This emphasis on people-centered and trauma-informed leadership can provide needed support and stability when others may be experiencing tremendous vulnerability, grief, and loss.

Furthermore, in the spirit of renewal and healing, post-crisis leadership demands a commitment to promote the dignity and worth of all people and an orientation to servant leadership that "can help make whole those with whom they come into contact" (Spears, 2002, p. 2). With an eye toward the generative potential of post-crisis leadership, this chapter provides an overview of several streams of relevant literature in the areas of humanity, dialogue, and an ethic of care; the discourse of renewal; and trauma-informed leadership. It concludes with various applications and strategies for exercising post-crisis leadership in the college and university context.

Foregrounding Humanity, Dialogue, and an Ethic of Care

The focus on foregrounding humanity, dialogue, and an ethic of care in the aftermath of crisis requires us to differentiate crisis leadership from crisis management. Crises threaten individual and organizational reputations, and much of the writing in the public relations and crisis management literature continues to center on issues related to impression management, image restoration, and strategies for preserving one's reputation. Crisis leadership moves beyond reputation and toward an ethic of care. There is no doubt that reputation management is an important component of any leader's role during a crisis; however, focusing exclusively on one's reputation has the potential to overlook other leadership factors considered to be most essential during these moments of collective disruption. Crisis leadership involves prevention and management, consistency and clarity, trust and transparency—with communication playing a critical role throughout each phase of any given crisis (Gigliotti, 2019). When crises strike, members of a group, team, or organization often seek guidance from those engaged in leadership—and it is incumbent on leaders to respond

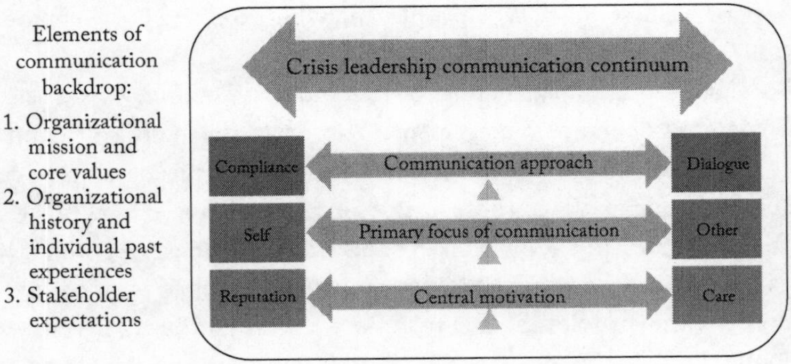

Elements of communication backdrop:

1. Organizational mission and core values
2. Organizational history and individual past experiences
3. Stakeholder expectations

FIG. 3. Based on Gigliotti (2019).

in ways that privilege the well-being of those most directly impacted by a given crisis.

As depicted in figure 3, one might analyze and deconstruct leadership communication in the aftermath of crisis using a continuum ranging from compliance to dialogue, from self-focus to other-focus, and from reputation to care (Gigliotti, 2019). This heuristic encourages a focus on the content of a leader's response to a crisis, along with a consideration of the leader's relationships with followers, their understanding of organizational history and the experience of the organization and/or leadership team with previous crises, and a recognition of the precedent-setting nature of leadership communication. At the heart of this framework is an emphasis on adopting approaches to crisis leadership that promote authentic, values-centered dialogue. Such a shift requires not just "talking to" but "talking with," as leaders engage in meaningful dialogue with key audiences in ways that enhance learning, build trust, and promote well-being and care.

Leadership decisions, actions, and behaviors have the potential to take on a heightened significance during times of crisis. These activities are subject to greater scrutiny and may have an oversized influence on how people respond to the crisis. Leadership influence extends beyond the crisis and spills into the post-crisis phase. The material, symbolic, and emotional impact of those engaged in leadership during times of crisis is the subject of much research (Boin & 't Hart, 2003; Boin et al., 2017; Hannah et al., 2009; James & Wooten, 2010; James et al., 2011; Stern, 2009), and consistent with the dominant themes presented in this book, leadership becomes especially critical during these moments of exigency. Crises are often characterized by extreme conditions, which frequently invoke a desire for calm, measured, and principled approaches to leadership to counter acute and often disorienting environmental factors. Crisis leadership requires a commitment to perspective-taking and active listening (James & Wooten, 2022). When crises strike, and in the period that follows, leadership presence becomes paramount, along with a willingness to expose one's humanity in a way that demonstrates an authentic ethic of care.

By way of example, I recall an interview I conducted with the president of a private, religiously affiliated institution in 2015 as part of a broader study exploring presidential leadership and the discursive and retrospective construction of leadership in crisis (Gigliotti, 2016). The president shared details regarding a major ice storm that impacted his heavily wooded suburban campus, which stretched over nearly two hundred acres. Describing the impact as "devastating," the ice storm resulted in loss of both power and hot water for three days immediately prior to the start of final exams. He went on to describe the details of the case:

> I have got 2,000 kids on a campus where trees are falling left and right. You know, it was just incredible. In a period of about twelve hours, it sounded like a war zone on this campus where trees were falling, limbs were falling, wires were coming down. The next morning it looked like a tornado had hit. It was just unbelievable. . . . You know [this storm] started in the evening at about 10:00 at night and it went till about 5:00 in the morning. And, uh, really all night I mean I was just lying there, like if anybody is outside, they are going to get killed by one of these trees because it happens instantaneously.

The president went on to outline his primary role in reassuring the students on campus and the families back home "that everything was under control and that we were taking care of their sons and daughters and we were making provisions and things of that nature." He also described the inherent communication difficulties the storm caused: "So, really the key questions there were number one, how do you keep the students safe? What do you do with 2,000 people on a campus that has no utilities whatsoever? Um, you are about to start final exams. Um, how do you communicate to parents when there is no way to communicate because everything is down? You know [*laughs*], you know why don't we send an email out to everybody [*laughs*], but you can't! And even how do you communicate with the students on campus?" As he further described the leadership implications at play in this incident, we can see how a sense of humanity and an authentic ethic of care converge in his response to the crisis:

> We took care of them. Most of the kids congregated in the dining hall because we had generators there. So, I basically made sure that I was visible there for them so that they could see that I was there. My presence . . . that they could come up and ask questions. You know, I could fill them in, that kind of thing was very, very important. I went to the residence hall where all the kids were placed just to make sure they were doing OK. You know, the presence is the key thing and the reassuring thing. I think that when you are dealing with students particularly on a campus that is basically residential, you've got to be that calming, reassuring presence so that everything remains as close to normal as possible and they don't start to get panicky.

Both the performative and human aspects of leadership are relevant for individuals seeking to demonstrate crisis leadership (Gigliotti, 2016)—and both require a commitment to engaging in meaningful dialogue with individuals impacted by a crisis.

Dialogue involves the creation of shared meaning between people whereby individuals "create something new together" as a result of their interaction (Bohm, 1996, p. 3). The description of dialogue provided by Cuentas and Méndez (2013) is especially relevant during interactions that have the potential to be highly charged or highly sensitive, such as those that may occur in the period that follows a crisis: "Dialogue is a process of genuine interaction in which human beings listen deeply and respectfully to each other in a way that what they learn changes them. Each participant in a dialogue strives to incorporate the concerns of the other participants into their own perspective, even when they continue to disagree. No participant gives up his or her identity, but each recognizes the human value of the claims of the others and therefore acts differently towards others" (p. 9). Dialogue is a critical condition for the practice of servant leadership (Gigliotti & Dwyer, 2016), and when dealing with the trauma, loss, or uncertainty that might accompany a crisis, the leader as servant may be a useful archetype for demonstrating care, compassion, and a commitment to the whole person. These practices can help to advance renewal, a topic that will be described more fully in the next section.

Discourse of Renewal

Ulmer (2001), noting a tendency in the scholarly and professional literature "for organizations to emphasize their own concerns over those of stakeholders" (p. 608), introduced the discourse of renewal theory as a way to underscore the centrality of stakeholders in crisis communication. At the time the theory was introduced—and indeed still today—there was a preoccupation with image repair, image management, image restoration, and corporate apologia—practices associated with defending an organization and repairing and restoring the reputation of the organization impacted by a crisis (Pyle et al., 2020; Seeger & Padgett, 2010; Seeger & Ulmer,

2002; Ulmer & Sellnow, 2002; Ulmer et al., 2007). Ulmer et al. (2007) introduce four primary characteristics of renewal:

1. Post-crisis communication is provisional as opposed to strategic. As the authors note, "Instead of developing responses designed to achieve some strategic outcome such as protecting the organization's image or escaping blame, renewal discourse is a more natural and immediate response to an event" (p. 131).
2. Renewal is prospective and forward-looking, rather than retrospective.
3. In a manner that is inherently optimistic, organizational leaders focus on the organization's ability to "reconstitute itself and capitalize on the opportunities embedded within the crisis" (p. 132).
4. Describing leaders as "instrumental forces for renewal and overcoming crisis" (p. 132), renewal is leader-based and relies on strong pre-crisis leadership that will allow leaders to draw upon a favorable reputation and "reservoir of goodwill" during times of crisis.

Viewed by some as a necessary corrective, crises possess the conditions for both danger and opportunity, and they have the potential to result in positive consequences for an organization or community. From the perspective of chaos theory, as Seeger and Ulmer (2002) summarize, the disruptions caused by crises may serve as natural points of bifurcation in the operation of complex, nonlinear systems (Murphy, 1996). As Butz (1997) writes, "Out of a chaos a new stability forms. In fact, it appears that a chaotic period is necessary for a new adaptive stability to be achieved" (p. 129). According to Seeger and Ulmer (2002), "The disorganization and chaos of crisis may be necessary to the order and structure of business as usual" (p. 129)—moments in time that allow for a reconsideration of outdated assumptions, structures, and paradigms. The crisis, or bifurcation as described in chaos theory, disrupts or significantly alters a system, and the process of renewal allows a community or organization to self-organize in response to this disruption (Seeger & Sellnow, 2016, p. 81). Communication during this post-crisis period can play an especially influential role in helping to frame these moments of exigency as "more dynamic, natural, and potentially positive processes in organizing" (Seeger & Ulmer, 2002, p. 129). Ultimately, it is the crisis that may lead to some positive outcome. Consider, for example, the ways in which groups, organizations, or communities come together and experience some degree of solidarity in the aftermath of collective trauma, or the policy changes that might result from crisis that help to improve the safety and well-being of others.

Unlike blame narratives, which are often contentious accounts focused on what occurred in the past, leaders, emergency management professionals, or individuals who experience a crisis will often turn to renewal narratives as a way of looking ahead to what might have never been. As Seeger and Sellnow (2016) write, "The renewal narrative develops after a crisis has created severe disruption to a region, community, or organization. Often basic elements of the establishment have been swept away and components of order and organization, including people, processes, and structures, are gone or no longer function as they have in the past" (p. 81). In responses to these moments of ruin, loss, or disruption, the stories of renewal that emerge may focus on the meaning of the crisis—a component of post-crisis leadership discussed in chapter 4—in addition to emphasizing opportunities for learning, growth, and improvement (Seeger & Sellnow, 2016). These narratives have the potential to rally others around a shared sense of hope for the future, and leaders may draw upon them in order to call others to action, acknowledge the unifying purpose and values of an organization, or create a compelling and inspiring vision for tomorrow (Seeger & Sellnow, 2016).

In their writing on the crisis renewal discourse that followed the tragic shooting at Sandy Hook Elementary School in 2012, Wombacher et al. (2018) describe renewal "not as a strategy to be utilized, but rather as a natural or provisional process that is more likely to emerge under some conditions" (p. 165). Certainly, not all crises contribute to organizational renewal and healing—and at times, what might be considered renewal for some may come at the loss of others, perpetuating injustices and inequalities in ways that further erode trust, well-being, or justice for members of a community. This leads us to consider the conditions that might contribute to successful renewal discourse, such as those outlined in Seeger and Ulmer (2002), Seeger et al. (2024), and Ulmer et al. (2009). Renewal discourse is likely to be more successful

(a) when crises are caused by natural disasters or other destructive means, because they provide an opportunity to rebuild
(b) when strong relationships are developed before a crisis, because stakeholders are more likely to commit to an organization they already know during the rebuilding process
(c) when an organization is able to take meaningful action and make observable changes to demonstrate commitment to improving the organization
(d) when organizational leaders have the ability to influence the stakeholders' frame of the crisis (Ulmer et al., 2009)

Adding the location of the crisis as one of these conditions, Wombacher et al. (2018) suggest that "the more relevant the location of a crisis is, the more likely it is that renewal can take place" (p. 166).

Going so far as to describe renewal as a moral imperative, Peiritsch (2019) writes that "renewal discourse not only suggests that organizations *ought to* reconceive crises as opportunities for growth, but it also implies that organizations are *morally obliged* to enact organizational change—regardless of the outcome" (p. 222). As a form of post-crisis healing, renewal allows stakeholders impacted by the crisis "to reconstitute themselves and move past the crisis" (Seeger et al., 2003, p. 148). Although renewal is prospective and forward-looking, recent writing on the subject points to the ways in which leaders and organizations might rely on past identity anchors as a way of navigating the post-crisis period (Anderson & Guo, 2020; Lambiase & English, 2021). Furthermore, suggesting that the discourse of renewal is amenable to both discursive and non-discursive symbols, Veil et al. (2011) write about the Oklahoma City National Memorial that honors the victims, survivors, rescuers, and all affected by the Oklahoma City bombing on April 19, 1995. The authors see it as an exemplar for how memorials, through the shared experience of grief, communicate renewal. As they note, "The memorial creates a context of peace and comfort that allows visitors from across the country and all over the world to remember the victims and experience the emotional healing that is a universal component of the indomitable human spirit. Healing leads to finding optimism in the midst of tragedy" (p. 179).

The discourse of renewal theory has been applied to a wide range of cases and contexts, including school shootings (Thompson et al., 2017; Wombacher et al., 2018), natural disasters (Lambiase & English, 2021; D. D. Sellnow et al., 2017), racial unrest and race-oriented crises (Peiritsch, 2019; Slagle et al., 2022), political crises (J. S. Smith, 2018), financial crises (Anderson & Guo, 2020), acts of terrorism (Ulmer & Sellnow, 2002; Veil et al., 2011), ethnic conflicts (Herovic & Veil, 2015), environmental crises (Ulmer & Pyle, 2021), and manufacturer recall crises (Anderson, 2012). In addition to these studies of organizational and community responses to crises, several studies have introduced scales to measure post-crisis communication (Xu, 2018) and organizational readiness for renewal (Fuller et al., 2019). Xu's (2018) post-crisis communication scale revealed four factors, including engagement, prospective focus, communication efficiency, and culture and value. The study noted that renewing discourse successfully predicted trust, commitment, satisfaction, and control mutuality. Building upon Xu's work, Fuller et al. (2019) found several communication indicators of an organization's pre-crisis readiness for renewal, depicted in

TABLE 5 Items Associated with Organizational Readiness for Renewal

EFFECTIVE ORGANIZATIONAL RHETORIC	ETHICAL COMMUNICATION
• We are seen as a model in our industry for resolving problems.	• In general, people in my organization live by our values.
• In the event of a problem, our communication is a model for organizations in our field and beyond to follow.	• My organization's values are clearly conveyed to our members.
• Generally, we are effective at getting our stakeholders to see problems in a similar light.	• On the whole, my organization has a "reservoir of goodwill" with external stakeholders it can draw on in the event of a problem.
• We are capable of convincing our collaborators to stick with us through a problematic event.	• We have a process in place that helps to resolve competing values about what information to share.
• Our communication about a negative event usually expresses a silver lining.	• When communicating with the public about a potential harm, we provide information about what can be done to protect oneself.
• In my organization we embrace failure as an opportunity to learn.	• When a problem arises that our organization is involved in, our messages express concern for those who are affected.
• Throughout a crisis event, my organization remains hopeful.	• We put steps in place to avoid similar issues when another organization confronts a negative event.
• My organization views crises as turning points that have the potential for future positive outcomes.	

SOURCE: Fuller et al. (2019).

table 5. Those engaged in leadership across higher education may consider each of the factors presented in the figure in determining their readiness for renewal in relation to both effective organizational rhetoric and the practice of ethical communication.

The evolving research on this topic often points back to a central theme detailed in Ulmer at al. (2019): "Crises do not build character; they expose the character of the organization" (p. 26). Leaders across higher education can play an important role in shepherding the renewal process in the aftermath of crisis in a way that moves beyond blame and image repair and restoration and toward healing and regeneration. When facing the spotlight of crisis and the heightened scrutiny that will likely accompany such moments, resolute leaders can reveal and reinforce the mission, values, and character of their institution in ways that help those affected by the crisis to recover and look ahead toward what might have never been had it not been for the experience. College and university leaders may choose to lean on professed ideals in supporting the victims of crisis in ways that promote the common good, advance equity, and model an obligation to the humanity of others.

Trauma-Informed Leadership

The converging crises of recent years have led to a greater focus on issues related to burnout, wellness, and well-being across higher education. According to research conducted by Gallup, only about one in four U.S. employees feel strongly that their organization cares about their well-being (Clifton & Harter, 2023). A 2022 Gallup poll found that educators reported the highest level of burnout of any industry, and 35 percent of college and university workers reported "always" or "very often" feeling burned out at work. In June 2015, the University of British Columbia co-hosted the International Conference on Health Promoting Universities and Colleges at their Okanagan campus, bringing together participants from forty-five countries, representing both educational institutions and health organizations, including the World Health Organization and UNESCO. Over three days, these organizations collaborated on the development of the Okanagan Charter: An International Charter for Health Promoting Universities and Colleges (University of British Columbia, n.d.). The charter offers a common language, principles, and framework for schools to adopt in their effort to create a campus that promotes health and well-being. At the time of this writing, nearly a hundred colleges have joined the network and agreed to embed good health into all aspects of campus culture across administration, operations, and faculty, in addition to leading health promotion action and collaboration locally and globally (University of British Columbia, n.d.). In describing the unique role of higher education, the guidance put forward in the charter elevates the broader impact of colleges and universities in the development of others:

> Higher education plays a central role in all aspects of the development of individuals, communities, societies and cultures—locally and globally. Higher education has a unique opportunity and responsibility to provide transformative education, engage the student voice, develop new knowledge and understanding, lead by example, and advocate to decision-makers for the benefit of society. In the emergent knowledge society, higher education institutions are positioned to generate, share, and implement knowledge and research findings to enhance health of citizens and communities both now and in the future. (University of British Columbia, n.d., p. 5)

In what ways might this charter serve as a guide for leadership in the aftermath of a crisis? In addition to highlighting the role of colleges and universities as exemplars for other sectors, the language of the charter advocates for a systems approach that embeds health throughout the entire organization. When dealing with the loss, grief, or trauma that might accompany crises, this focus on the well-being of *all* members of a community becomes a topic of widespread concern. The systems perspective allows us to consider not only what leaders say and how they behave, but also the broader policy and structural changes that might be enacted to promote and ensure the well-being of others in the aftermath of trauma.

Writing for the *Harvard Business Review* in the aftermath of the 9/11 attacks, Dutton et al. (2002) discuss the importance of leading in times of trauma:

> The managerial rule books fail us at times like these, when people are searching for meaning and a reason to hope for the future. There is, however, something leaders can do in times of collective pain and confusion. By the very nature of your position, you can help individuals and companies begin to heal

by taking actions that demonstrate your own compassion, thereby unleashing a compassionate response throughout the whole organization. . . . Indeed, we've found that a leader's ability to enable a compassionate response throughout a company directly affects the organization's ability to maintain high performance in difficult times. It fosters a company's capacity to heal, to learn, to adapt, and to excel. (pp. 55, 56)

As the authors go on to note, at any time in the life an organization, individual or collective grief is inevitable; and although one cannot eliminate the suffering of others, the demonstration of trauma-informed leadership can encourage the healing process. Leaders can stimulate renewal by taking the time to mourn for what might have been lost and to look ahead in pursuit of possibilities that have yet to be realized. By modeling compassion and empathy in the period to follow a crisis, leaders can deepen their connection with individuals experiencing grief, loss, or trauma.

Writing specifically about the role of therapists, Milner and Echterling (2021) put forward guidance that certainly extends into the domain of trauma-informed leadership: "It is important for therapists to remember that the act of bearing witness as an empathetic, attuned, active listener is a powerful intervention in and of itself" (p. 300). Of course, the role of the leader may not, cannot, and should not replace the type of support that is required of licensed mental health professionals. However, it is incumbent on leaders to help provide stability for those impacted by a crisis and to help navigate a path forward in the aftermath of loss. This renewal process, rooted in trauma-informed leadership, is one that extends over a long period of time.

In discussing the practice of trauma-informed leadership, Koloroutis and Pole (2021) articulate the importance of four relational practices—attuning, wondering, following, and holding—each of which is discussed further in table 6. Advocating for visible, emotionally present, and accessible leaders who listen, prepare, support, and care for their teams during traumatic events,

TABLE 6 Four Relational Practices

PRACTICE	MEANING	LANGUAGE
Attuning	• Practice of human connection • Shutting out distractions, focusing attention, and listening • Being present • Noticing	• Thank you for coming to me . . . • I feel honored that you would share . . . • It makes sense you would feel . . .
Wondering	• Practice of curiosity and genuine interest • Suspending judgment and assumptions • Noticing • Listening	• How are you . . . really? • What worries you? • What's most important to you? • What do you need?
Following	• Practice of quiet listening • Staying with what we hear and notice • Being in the moment • Allowing expression of emotions	• Tell me more about . . . • Do I have this right? • What's most important to you right now?
Holding	• Practice of creating a safe space • Doing what we said we would do • Remembering what we've been told • Taking the right action • Listening without defense • Honoring boundaries	• I remember when you told me . . . • I'll follow through and make sure . . . • Thank you for being open and vulnerable with me . . . • I'm here.

SOURCE: Koloroutis & Pole (2021, p. 33).

the model is one that also proves useful as the dust settles after a crisis and as members of a community begin to heal.

Higher Education Applications

The various streams of literature summarized in this chapter establish the contours of a road map for leaders to consider when seeking to advance renewal in the aftermath of crisis. Some of these tactics include demonstrating one's humanity, engaging in an ethic of care, cultivating opportunities for meaningful dialogue, listening to others with an intent to understand, drawing upon the discourse of renewal, and practicing trauma-based leadership. These tactics take on a heightened significance during extreme periods, such as when responding to institutional or environmental crises. In particular, ongoing pressures related to employee burnout, workplace inequities, racial injustice, and public skepticism about the value of higher education make the focus of this chapter one of great contemporary importance for those interested in the study and practice of leadership in higher education.

We could turn our attention to various examples of colleges and universities seeking to advance renewal in the aftermath of crisis. In some cases, such as in the 2022 fatal stabbing of four University of Idaho students in their residence located blocks away from the campus, the healing process involved the elimination of the physical property where the crime occurred. As the University of Idaho president, Scott Green, announced in his press conference: "This is a healing step and removes the physical structure where the crime that shook our community was committed. Demolition also removes efforts to further sensationalize the crime scene" (Alsharif, 2023). As Green went on to note, "We will never forget Xana, Ethan, Madison and Kaylee, and I will do everything in my power to protect their dignity and respect their memory" (Alsharif, 2023).

In the case of the deadly shooting at Michigan State University (MSU) on February 13, 2023, the healing process involved the cancellation of classes for a week and the decision to return to normal operations after this time period. In his article for *Inside Higher Ed*, entitled "After the Smoke Clears, When Should Classes Resume?," Knox (2023) details the tension surrounding this decision to return to normal academic routines shortly after this tragedy. As quoted in the article, Becca Smith, president of the American College Counseling Association, said that "in the wake of a campuswide tragedy, institutions shouldn't wait too long to reintroduce academic life. At the same time, it's vital that they don't move on too quickly and force students back into situations that could be retraumatizing" (Knox, 2023). "That routine does help give a sense of, 'We're going to be OK.' But it's also important to take time to sit with the fear and grief and not avoid that and pretend like everything is normal," Smith said. "It's a struggle to find that balance" (Knox, 2023). As Knox continues, "MSU officials didn't want to make students revisit the sites of the shootings: the Student Union and Berkey Hall, where the three killings took place, have been shut down for the remainder of the semester. Hundreds of classes normally scheduled in those buildings have been relocated, some to rooms that are not traditionally used for classes." As noted in both cases, the decision to advance renewal may involve changes to policies, practices, and structures in order to signal a commitment to the healing process. Furthermore, as illustrated in the MSU case, the healing process takes time and competing perspectives may exist regarding the appropriate timing by which an institution moves forward in the aftermath of a tragedy.

The murder of George Floyd, discussed at the opening of this chapter, along with the murders of Ahmaud Arbery, Breonna Taylor, and other unarmed Black men and women at the hands of American police sparked global unrest and a broader conversation regarding issues of racial justice. College and university leaders across the country spoke out against these killings and in support of efforts to dismantle racism. In a report published by the National Association of Student Personnel Administrators (NASPA), the professional organization for student affairs administrators, and the National Association of Diversity Officers in Higher Education, Chamberlain et al. (2021) found that 230 colleges and universities (from a sample of three hundred NASPA member institutions) issued statements in the two-week period following Floyd's death. Writing for *Inside Higher Ed*, Whitford (2021) shared a key finding that "six in 10 of the statements included mentions of discrimination against the Black and/or African American community, while just over half discussed institutional or structural racism." In the spirit of renewal and rooted in a broader commitment to inquiry and the common good, institutions of higher education have also engaged in new initiatives and enacted new policies to correct long-standing inequities. These actions can be organized into seven categories: (1) resource investment, (2) hiring and recruitment, (3) education or training, (4) data assessment, (5) pedagogy, (6) public statues and buildings, and (7) campus police reform (Chamberlain et al., 2021). For example, funded by a $15 million grant from the Andrew W. Mellon Foundation and in support of the institution's broader commitment to cultivating a beloved community, Rutgers University launched its Institute for the Study of Global Racial Justice that brings together scholars from across the university to use humanistic theories, methods, and approaches to study global issues of race and social justice (Rutgers University, n.d.). As articulated by founding executive director Michelle Stephens, "The hope here is that by drawing upon expertise across all fields of the humanities, from law to language, from philosophy to history and gender studies, the institute will stand at the forefront in helping to inform policies to confront and address global inequity, injustice, racism and intolerance. It will also be accomplished through artistic and cultural endeavors that encourage imaginative solutions for influencing public opinion and inspiring cultural transformations."

The renewal process may also involve the removal or installation of memorials to maintain collective memory (Veil et al., 2021); expand, enrich, or preserve our awareness of past crises; or address issues of historical significance now under scrutiny. For example, following the murder of Floyd, the Southern Poverty Law Center reported that 157 Confederate memorials were removed in the United States in 2020—the most in one year (Rhoden & Paul, 2022). These include the removal of three plaques commemorating students who fought for the Confederate Army at the University of Alabama, the movement of a campus monument to the Confederacy at the University of

Mississippi to a secluded Civil War cemetery, and the removal of the Rebels team mascot at the University of Nevada, Las Vegas, in response to concerns expressed by a Native American student association. In the case of building a memorial to advance renewal, we may consider the semicircle of stones at Virginia Tech installed in honor and memory of the victims of the 2007 campus shooting. As described on the memorial's website, "Hokie Stone has long symbolized the foundation of Virginia Tech. Now, it also symbolizes our relentless spirit, our courage to move forward, and our determination never to forget" (Virginia Tech, n.d.). In another example, on the campus of Kent State University a memorial commemorates the events of May 4, 1970, when four students were killed and nine were wounded during an anti-war protest on the campus. According to the university's website, the memorial is "constructed of car-nelian granite, a stone associated with strength and time" and "surrounded by 58,175 daffodils, the number of the country's losses in Vietnam" (Kent State University, n.d.). Furthermore, "engraved in the plaza's stone threshold are the words 'Inquire, Learn, Reflect.' The inscription, agreed upon by the designer and Kent State University, affirms the intent that the memorial site provide visitors an opportunity to inquire into the many rea-sons and purposes of the events, to encourage a learning process, and to reflect on how differences may be resolved peacefully" (Kent State University, n.d.).

Considerations for Post-Crisis Leadership Action

The work of advancing renewal following periods of exigency requires persistence, strength, and humility, along with a deeply rooted commitment to supporting those most directly affected by the crisis. The impact of such efforts can lead to individual and collective transformation. As Walsh (2007) writes, "Learning and growthful change out of tragic loss can spark new and renewed commitments and priorities. Recovery is a journey of the heart and spirit, bringing survivors back to the fullness of life" (p. 213). Informed by the examples and themes presented in this chapter, leaders might consider the following considerations for post-crisis renewal:

- Demonstrate trauma-informed leadership behaviors in ways that build trust, including respect for the individual, active listening, presence, and empathy.
- Encourage renewal in one-on-one settings and in settings involving groups, teams, and the broader community.
- Respond in ways that demonstrate an understanding of the often disproportionate impact of crises on members of a community.
- Respect the need for individual and collective healing, and the ways in which this effort occurs in both private and public settings.
- Create opportunities for physical, social, emotional, and spiritual healing in ways that seem most appropriate given the scale of the crisis, the impact on institutional stakeholders, and the institutional setting.
- Participate in memorial rituals and vigils, along with celebrations of key milestones, in order to facilitate individual and collective healing.
- Forge linkages between renewal activities and the organization's ethos, mission, and values.

The sense of loss that can accompany crisis may be attributed to the incident itself, and it might also be amplified by a perceived criticism in the leadership response to the incident. These critical and high-stakes moments often present leaders with difficult choices, and their response to these issues (or the decision to withhold a public response) can cause anger and hurt among key audiences. In these cases, perceptions of effective or ineffective leadership in the midst of crisis can spill over and impact one's credibility during the post-crisis period. The advancement of renewal and healing requires an acknowledgment of the pain, a receptivity to forgive, and a desire to move forward.

Understandably, in the aftermath of loss, trauma, or erosion of trust, these conditions will often take time and a sincere willingness to repair relationships or restore confidence. Ironically, the healing process can cause pain, or as author Toni Morrison (2007) wrote in her novel, *Beloved*, "Anything dead coming back to life hurts." In recognition of these difficulties, the progress of renewal in post-crisis leadership requires vulnerability, compassion, and patience.

Conclusion

Writing on the subject of crisis proves to be a difficult undertaking, especially given the evolving dynamics of contemporary cases and the emergence of new crises. At the time of writing, for example, the impact of COVID-19 continues to recede from view—and a new set of storylines and challenges consume the attention of higher education leaders, such as the unfolding global conflict in the Middle East and the ripple effect on college and university campuses, the financial threat imposed by declining student enrollment, the growing impact of artificial intelligence, and the dismantling of diversity, equity, and inclusion efforts across the United States. Indeed, the stage seems to be set for higher education to serve as a partisan wedge issue in the 2024 elections and the period to follow. In light of these evolving incidents and the inevitable crises that lie ahead, leadership in higher education demands a thoughtful, measured, and inclusive approach. As jointly constructed by leaders, followers, and the contexts in which individuals are embedded, leadership dynamics are fluid, lively, and in a continual state of flux—and crises certainly add a layer of complexity for those seeking to lead in this current climate. Indeed, crises amplify and accentuate the need for effective leadership, and as the examples detailed in this book help to illustrate, this need extends into the post-crisis period. As we reach the conclusion of this exploration into post-crisis leadership, the following conclusions may be particularly useful for those interested in the study and practice of resilience, renewal, and reinvention in the aftermath of disruption:

- The period following a crisis is a time of uncertainty and ambiguity—and is also one of possibility. This moment in time is ripe for individual and collective learning, recovery, and growth—and the ways in which leaders approach this stage of a crisis may have implications for how they are viewed and perceived during the next inevitable crisis.
- Post-crisis leadership is not an event, but a process. It is both an ongoing and variable process that is directly shaped by the conditions of the crisis that preceded it and the institutional and environmental variables at play during its aftermath.
- Post-crisis leadership is socially constructed. In much the same way as crises are socially constructed and influenced by the perceptions of individuals impacted by the event or series of events, what constitutes "post-crisis" is also subjective and may possess different meanings for different people. Thus, the expectations for and evaluation of post-crisis leadership effectiveness lie in the eyes of the beholder.
- Post-crisis leadership is inherently unpredictable—and yet predictably important. Although one cannot predict how long an organization might endure the challenges associated with any given crisis, it is a safe bet to consider the post-crisis period as a decisive one for how leaders will be evaluated in the future.

As I hope is clear from my treatment of the topic in the book, the focus on post-crisis leadership is not meant to downplay the importance of crisis and risk prevention or the need for effective leadership during these crucible moments. Rather, with so much attention centered on pre-crisis and crisis considerations, there is a need to reassert the importance of post-crisis leadership. By entering into conversation with relevant streams of literature across diverse fields, I hope the assumptions, concepts, and strategies detailed throughout this text help to inform the study and practice of post-crisis leadership, particularly in the context of higher education. Finally, by purposefully highlighting the interactions across leaders, followers, and context—along with exploring the intersections and interdependencies across the practices proposed in the post-crisis leadership framework—the ideas discussed in this book aim to advance a systems view of post-crisis leadership, one that is relational, values-oriented, and rooted in communication.

As we see time and again in the crises that befall colleges and universities, what one person might describe as "post-crisis" may be another's crisis. Although the media attention may subside, the impact of a crisis may linger in the days, weeks, months, and years to follow. A formulaic approach to diagnosing crisis and any attempt to measure the distance between crisis and post-crisis is fraught with difficulty, particularly given the subjectivity associated with such efforts. Rather than impose a prescriptive model for the work of post-crisis leadership, the theory-informed framework presented throughout this book is meant to serve as a guide for leaders to consider during this period of great consequence. The practices detailed in the framework often overlap, and leaders may find it helpful to consider the extent to which these five practices resonate with their unique challenges and experiences. Finally, a consideration of these five practices helps to underscore a significant point for anyone seeking to engage in this work: *Effective leadership before, during, and certainly in the aftermath of crisis requires intentionality, along with a focus on communication, an understanding of enduring principles and values, and a deeply rooted commitment to people-centered ways of being.* Individuals naturally crave stability and hope, and the pressures of crisis and the period following it demand approaches to leadership that can take stock of historical conditions, address the needs of the moment, and encourage the community to look ahead to a brighter future with clarity, confidence, and conviction.

Acknowledgments

It is with sincere appreciation that I recognize the following individuals and groups for their contributions to this book.

To my colleagues at Rutgers University and across higher education who helped me to think critically about the importance of post-crisis leadership as both a concept and a set of applied practices that could advance the work of our institutions.

To my family and friends who offered their love and support following the tragic passing of my mother. My work on this project was inspired in many ways by her loss. The encouragement from family and friends provided me with the courage and confidence to move forward in a way that would undoubtedly make her proud.

To Peggy Solic, senior editor at Rutgers University Press, for her enthusiastic support of this project, and to the entire team at Rutgers University Press and Westchester Publishing Services for their responsiveness and professionalism.

To Karen Verde, freelance editor at Green Pelican Editorial Services, for her prompt, thorough, and constructive guidance throughout the copyediting process.

To Rebecca Arends, graduate coordinator in our Office of Organizational Leadership at Rutgers University, for her assistance in researching COVID-19-related communication across the Big Ten member universities.

To Angie Miccinello for her timely completion of the index for this book.

References

Abrams, Z. (2022, September 1). Stress of mass shootings causing cascade of collective traumas. *Monitor on Psychology*. https://www.apa.org /monitor/2022/09/news-mass-shootings-collective-traumas

Alexander, B. (2013, September 18). *Peak education 2013*. Bryan Alexander. https://bryanalexander.org/uncategorized/peak-education-2013/

Alexander, B. (2018, May 22). *American higher education enrollment declined. Again*. Bryan Alexander. https://bryanalexander.org/enrollment /american-higher-education-enrollment-declined-again/

Allen, K. E. (2018). *Leading from the roots: Nature-inspired leadership lessons for today's world*. Morgan James.

Allen, S. J., Shankman, M. L., & Haber-Curran, P. (2016). Developing emotionally intelligent leadership: The need for deliberate practice and collaboration across disciplines. *New Directions for Higher Education, 174*, 79–91. https://doi.org/10.1002/he.20191

Alsharif, M. (2023, February 24). *House where four University of Idaho students were killed will be demolished*. Yahoo News. https://news.yahoo .com/house-where-four-university-idaho-224526567.html

Alvarez-Robinson, S. (2024, February 27). *How to face adversity and change in higher education with resilience*. Times Higher Education. https:// www.timeshighereducation.com/campus/how-face-adversity-and -change-higher-education-resilience

Alvesson, M., & Sveningsson, S. (2003). The great disappearing act: Difficulties in doing "leadership." *Leadership Quarterly, 14*(3), 359–381.

American Psychological Association. (2018). Resilience. In *APA dictionary of psychology*. https://dictionary.apa.org/resilience?_gl=1*1ncqwyl*_ga*NTk2NDAxMjc3LjE3MTA5NjUoNjI.*_ga_SZXLGDJGNB*MTcxMTEoMjEoOC42LjEuMTcxMTEoMjI1MC4wLjAuMA

Amico, L. (2022, December 29). Was 2022 the year of resilience? *Harvard Business Review*. https://hbr.org/2022/12/was-2022-the-year-of-resilience

Anderson, L. (2012). Recalling Toyota's crisis: Utilizing the discourse of renewal. *Journal of Professional Communication, 2*(1), 21–42. https://doi.org/10.15173/jpc.v2i1.112

Anderson, L. B., & Guo, J. (2020). Paradoxical timelines in Wells Fargo's crisis discourse: Expanding the discourse of renewal theory. *International Journal of Business Communication, 57*(2), 212–226. https://doi.org/10.1177/2329488419882761

Antonacopoulou, E. P., & Sheaffer, Z. (2014). Learning in crisis: Rethinking the relationship between organizational learning and crisis management. *Journal of Management Inquiry, 23*(1), 5–21. https://doi.org/10.1177/1056492612472730

Argyris, C. (1977, September). Double loop learning in organizations. *Harvard Business Review, 55*, 115–125.

Argyris, C. (1980). *Inner contradictions of rigorous research*. Academic Press.

Argyris, C. (1982). The executive mind and double-loop learning. *Organizational Dynamics, 11*(2), 5–22. https://doi.org/10.1016/0090-2616(82)90002-X

Argyris, C. (1990). *Overcoming organizational defenses: Facilitating organizational learning*. Allyn & Bacon.

Argyris, C. (1999). *On organizational learning* (2nd ed.). Wiley-Blackwell.

Argyris, C., & Schön, D. A. (1974). *Theory in practice: Increasing professional effectiveness*. Jossey-Bass.

Argyris, C., & Schön, D. A. (1978). *Organizational learning: A theory of action perspective*. Addison-Wesley.

Armstrong, J. H., & Frykberg, E. R. (2007). Lessons from the response to the Virginia Tech shootings. *Disaster Medicine and Public Health Perspectives, 1*(Suppl. 1), S7–S8. https://doi.org/10.1097/DMP.0b013e3181514969

Association of Public and Land-Grant Universities. (2020). *How COVID-19 changed everything and nothing at all.* https://www.aplu.org/June2020 ChallengesReport

Ayebi-Arthur, K. (2017). E-learning, resilience and change in higher education: Helping a university cope after a natural disaster. *E-Learning and Digital Media, 14*(5), 259–274. https://doi.org/10.1177 /2042753017751712

Bak, O. (2012). Universities: Can they be considered as learning organizations? A preliminary micro-level perspective. *Learning Organization, 19*(2), 163–172. https://doi.org/10.1108/09696471211201515

Baldwin, D. L. (2021, April 1). Higher education's racial reckoning reaches far beyond slavery. *The Washington Post.* https://www.washingtonpost .com/outlook/2021/04/01/higher-educations-racial-reckoning-reaches -far-beyond-slavery/

Barber, H. F. (1992). Developing strategic leadership: The US Army War College experience. *Journal of Management Development, 11*(6), 4–12. https://doi.org/10.1108/02621719210018208

Barbour, J. B., Buzzanell, P. M., Kinsella, W. J., & Stephens, K. K. (2018). Communicating/organizing for reliability, resilience, and safety: Special issue introduction. *Corporate Communications: An International Journal, 23*(2), 154–161. https://doi.org/10.1108/CCIJ-01-2018-0019

Bartunek, J., Krim, R. Necochea, R., & Humphries, M. (1999). Sense-making, sensegiving, and leadership in strategic organizational development. In J. Wagner (Ed.), *Advances in qualitative organizational research* (pp. 37–71). JAI Press.

Bass, B. M. (1985). *Leadership and performance beyond expectations.* Free Press.

Bass, B. M. (1998). *Transformational leadership: Industrial, military, and educational impact.* Lawrence Erlbaum Associates Publishers.

Beach, D. (2017). Process tracing methods in the social sciences. In *Oxford Research Encyclopedia.* https://doi.org/10.1093/acrefore/9780190228637 .013.176

Bennis, W., & Thomas, R. J. (2002, September). Crucibles of leadership. *Harvard Business Review.* https://hbr.org/2002/09/crucibles-of-leadership

Birnbaum, R., & Shushok, F. (2001). The "crisis" crisis in higher education: Is that a wolf or a pussycat at the academy's door? In P. G. Altbach,

P. J. Gumport, & D. B. Johnstone (Eds.), *In defense of American higher education* (pp. 59–84). Johns Hopkins University Press.

Block, J., & Kremen, A. M. (1996). IQ and ego-resiliency: Conceptual and empirical connections and separateness. *Journal of Personality and Social Psychology, 70*(2), 349–361. https://doi.org/10.1037/0022-3514.70.2.349

Bohm, D. (1996). *On dialogue.* Routledge.

Boin, A., & 't Hart, P. (2003). Public leadership in times of crisis: Mission impossible? *Public Administration Review, 63*(5), 544–553. https://doi.org/10.1111/1540-6210.00318

Boin, A., 't Hart, P., Stern, E., & Sundelius, B. (2017). *The politics of crisis management: Public leadership under pressure* (2nd ed.). Cambridge University Press. https://doi.org/10.1017/9781316339756

Bok, D. (2013). *Higher education in America* (2nd ed.). Princeton University Press.

Bonanno, G. A. (2004). Loss, trauma, and human resilience: Have we underestimated the human capacity to thrive after extremely aversive events? *American Psychologist, 59*(1), 20–28. https://doi.org/10.1037/0003-066X.59.1.20

Bonanno, G. A., Westphal, M., & Mancini, A. D. (2011). Resilience to loss and potential trauma. *Annual Review of Clinical Psychology, 7,* 511–535. https://doi.org/10.1146/annurev-clinpsy-032210-104526

Booker, L. (2014). Crisis management: Changing times for colleges. *Journal of College Admission*, no. 222, 16–23.

Bowman, R. (2002). The real work of department chair. *Clearing House, 75*(3), 158–162. https://doi.org/10.1080/00098650209599258

Bozkurt, A. (2022). Resilience, adaptability, and sustainability of higher education: A systematic mapping study on the impact of the coronavirus (COVID-19) pandemic and the transition to the new normal. *Journal of Learning for Development, 9*(1), 1–16. https://doi.org/10.56059/jl4d.v9i1.590

Brenan, M. (2023, July 11). *Americans' confidence in higher education down sharply.* Gallup. https://news.gallup.com/poll/508352/americans-confidence-higher-education-down-sharply.aspx

Brint, S. (2019, January 9). Is this higher education's golden age? *The Chronicle of Higher Education.* https://www.chronicle.com/article/is-this-higher-educations-golden-age/

Brockner, J., & James, E. H. (2008). Toward an understanding of when executives see crisis as opportunity. *Journal of Applied Behavioral Science, 44*(1), 94–115. https://doi.org/10.1177/0021886307313824

Bui, H. T. M., & Baruch, Y. (2010a). Creating learning organizations: A systems perspective. *Learning Organization, 17*(3), 208–227. https://doi.org/10.1108/09696471011034919

Bui, H. T. M., & Baruch, Y. (2010b). Creating learning organizations in higher education: Applying a systems perspective. *Learning Organization, 17*(3), 228–242. https://doi.org/10.1108/09696471011034928

Bui, H. T. M., & Baruch, Y. (2012). Learning organizations in higher education: An empirical evaluation within an international context. *Management Learning, 43*(5), 515–544. https://doi.org/10.1177/1350507611431212

Buller, J. L. (2012). *The essential department chair.* Jossey-Bass.

Buller, J. L. (2014). *Change leadership in higher education: A practical guide to academic transformation.* Jossey-Bass. https://doi.org/10.1002/9781119210825

Butz, M. (1997). *Chaos and complexity: Implications for psychological theory and practice.* Taylor & Francis.

Buzzanell, P. M. (2010). Resilience: Talking, resisting, and imagining new normalcies into being. *Journal of Communication, 60*(1), 1–14. https://doi.org/10.1111/j.1460-2466.2009.01469.x

Buzzanell, P. M. (2018). Organizing resilience as adaptive-transformational tensions. *Journal of Applied Communication Research, 46*(1), 14–18. https://doi.org/10.1080/00909882.2018.1426711\

Buzzanell, P. M., & Houston, J. B. (2018). Communication and resilience: Multilevel applications and insights—A *Journal of Applied Communication Research* Forum. *Journal of Applied Communication Research, 46*(1), 1–4. https://doi.org/10.1080/00909882.2017.1412086

Calcado, A. M., Gracias, V., Ruben, B. D., St. Pierre, J., & Strom, B. L. (2021). How one university harnessed internal knowledge and expertise to effectively combat the COVID-19 pandemic. *Electronic Journal of Knowledge Management, 20*(1), 1–16. https://doi.org/10.34190/ejkm.20.1.2439

Calhoun, L. G., & Tedeschi, R. G. (1999). *Facilitating posttraumatic growth: A clinician's guide.* Lawrence Erlbaum Associates Publishers. https://doi.org/10.4324/9781410602268

Calhoun, L. G., & Tedeschi, R. G. (2006). The foundations of posttraumatic growth: An expanded framework. In L. G. Calhoun & R. G. Tedeschi (Eds.), *Handbook of posttraumatic growth: Research and practice* (pp. 3–23). Lawrence Erlbaum Associates Publishers.

Cambridge University Press and Assessment. (n.d.). Reinvention. In *Cambridge dictionary*. Retrieved April 20, 2024, from https://dictionary.cambridge.org/us/dictionary/english/reinvention

Carmeli, A., & Schaubroeck, J. (2008). Organisational crisis-preparedness: The importance of learning from failures. *Long Range Planning, 41*(2), 177–196. https://doi.org/10.1016/j.lrp.2008.01.001

Chamberlain, A. W., Dunlap, J., & Russell, P. G. (2021, July 26). *Moving from words to action: The influence of racial justice statements on campus equity efforts.* NASPA. https://www.naspa.org/report/moving-from-words-to-action-the-influence-of-racial-justice-statements-on-campus-equity-efforts

Chewning, L. V., Lai, C.-H., & Doerfel, M. L. (2013). Organizational resilience and using information and communication technologies to rebuild communication structures. *Management Communication Quarterly, 27*(2), 237–263. https://doi.org/10.1177/0893318912465815

Chhikara, A., Osei-Tutu, A. A. Z., Zhou, L, Oudghiri, S., Dwomoh, R., & Bell, T. (2022). In times of crisis: Our story of resilience. *Journal of Critical Thought and Praxis, 11*(3), Article 6. https://doi.org/10.31274/jctp.13013

Chu, D. (2012). *The department chair primer* (2nd ed.). Jossey-Bass.

Clifton, J., & Harter, J. (2019). *It's the manager: Moving from boss to coach.* Gallup Press.

Clifton, J., & Harter, J. (2023). *Culture shock.* Simon & Schuster.

Cole, J. M., Leak, J. B., & Martinez, E. (Eds.). (2021). The pandemics of racism and COVID-19. *Journal of Higher Education Management, 36*(1). https://issuu.com/aaua10/docs/twin_pandemics/s/11997048

College and University Professional Association for Human Resources. (2022). *The CUPA-HR 2022 Higher Education Employee Retention Survey: Initial results.* https://www.cupahr.org/surveys/research-briefs/higher-ed-employee-retention-survey-findings-july-2022/

Coombs, W. T. (2022). *Ongoing crisis communication: Planning, managing, and responding* (6th ed.). Sage.

Corley, K. G., & Gioia, D. A. (2004). Identity ambiguity and change in the wake of a corporate spin-off. *Administrative Science Quarterly, 49*(2), 173–208. https://doi.org/10.2307/4131471

Crichton, M. T., Ramsay, C. G., & Kelly, T. (2009). Enhancing organizational resilience through emergency planning: Learnings from cross-sectoral lessons. *Journal of Contingencies and Crisis Management, 17*(1), 24–37. https://doi.org/10.1111/j.1468-5973.2009.00556.x

Cuentas, M. A., & Méndez, A. L. (2013). *Practical guide on democratic dialogue.* Crisis Prevention and Recovery Practice Area of the UNDP Regional Centre for Latin America and the Caribbean, and the Department of Sustainable Democracy and Special Missions of the Secretariat for Political Affairs of the General Secretariat of the Organization of American States.

Cunningham, T., & Pfeiffer, K. (2022). Posttraumatic growth as a model to measure and guide implementation of COVID-19 recovery and resiliency. *Nursing Administration Quarterly, 46*(1), 81–87. https://doi.org/10.1097/NAQ.0000000000000509

Daniels, M. (2021, January 4). *Annual open letter to the people of Purdue from Mitch Daniels.* Purdue University. https://www.purdue.edu/president/mitch-daniels/messages/annual-open-letters/2101-med-openletter-full.php

Daniels, M. (2022, January 5). *Annual open letter to the people of Purdue from Mitch Daniels.* Purdue University. https://purdue.edu/president/mitch-daniels/messages/annual-open-letters/2201-med-openletter-full.php

Denney, F. (2021). The "golden braid" model: Courage, compassion and resilience in higher education leadership. *Journal of Higher Education Policy and Leadership Studies, 2*(2), 37–49. https://doi.org/10.52547/johepal.2.2.37

Dervin, B. (1992). From the mind's eye of the user: The sense-making qualitative-quantitative methodology. In J. D. Glazier & R. P. Powell (Eds.), *Qualitative research in information management* (pp. 61–84). Libraries Unlimited.

Dervin, B. (1998). Sense-making theory and practice: An overview of user interests in knowledge seeking and use. *Journal of Knowledge Management, 2*(2), 36–46. https://doi.org/10.1108/13673279810249369

Devies, B., & Guthrie, K. L. (2024). Emerging from the fog: Reimagining leadership and generativity. *Journal of Leadership Studies*. https://doi.org /10.1002/jls.21892

Dewey, J. (1974). *John Dewey on education: Selected writings*. University of Chicago Press.

Dierkes, M., Berthoin Antal, A., Child, J., & Nonaka, I. (Eds.). (2001). *Handbook of organizational learning and knowledge*. Oxford University Press. https://doi.org/10.1093/oso/9780198295839.001.0001

Doerfel M. L., Lai C.-H., Chewning L. V. (2010). The evolutionary role of interorganizational communication: Modeling social capital in disaster contexts. *Human Communication Research*, *36*(2), 125–162. https://doi.org /10.1111/j.1468-2958.2010.01371.x

Doerfel, M. L., & Prezelj, I. (2017). Resilience in a complex and unpredict- able world. *Journal of Contingencies and Crisis Management*, *25*(3), 118–122. https://doi.org/10.1111/1468-5973.12177

DuBrin, A. J. (Ed.). (2013). *Handbook of research on crisis leadership in organizations*. Edward Elgar. https://doi.org/10.4337/9781781006405

Dunford, R., & Jones, D. (2000). Narrative in strategic change. *Human Relations*, *53*(9), 1207–1226. https://doi.org/10.1177/0018726700539005

Dutton, J. E., Frost, P. J., Worline, M. C., Lilius, J. M., & Kanov, J. M. (2002, January). Leading in times of trauma. *Harvard Business Review*. https://hbr.org/2002/01/leading-in-times-of-trauma

Dweck, C. S. (2008). *Mindset*. Ballantine Books.

Dwyer, G., Hardy, C., & Tsoukas, H. (2023). Struggling to make sense of it all: The emotional process of sensemaking following an extreme incident. *Human Relations*, *76*(3), 420–451. https://doi.org/10.1177/00187267211059464

Elliott, D. (2009). The failure of organizational learning from crisis— A matter of life and death? *Journal of Contingencies and Crisis Manage- ment*, *17*(3), 157–168. https://doi.org/10.1111/j.1468-5973.2009.00576.x

Entman, R. M. (1993). Framing: Toward clarification of a paradigm. *Journal of Communication*, *43*(4), 51–58. https://doi.org/10.1111/j.1460 -2466.1993.tb01304.x

Estes, C. L. (1983). Social security: The social construction of a crisis. *Milbank Memorial Fund Quarterly: Health and Society*, *61*(3), 445–461. https://doi.org/10.2307/3349867

Eury, J. L., Kreiner, G. E., Treviño, L. K., & Gioia, D. A. (2018). The past is not dead: Legacy identification and alumni ambivalence in the wake of the Sandusky scandal at Penn State. *Academy of Management Journal*, 61(3). https://doi.org/10.5465/amj.2015.0534

Fairhurst, G. T. (2009). Considering context in discursive leadership research. *Human Relations*, 62(11), 1607–1633. https://doi.org/10.1177/0018726709346379

Fairhurst, G. T., & Sarr, R. (1996). *The art of framing: Managing the language of leadership*. Jossey-Bass. https://doi.org/10.1093/ajhp/53.21.2670

Fernandez, F., Coulson, H., & Zou, Y. (2022). Leading in the eye of a storm: How one team of administrators exercised disaster resilience. *Higher Education*, 83(4), 929–944. https://doi.org/10.1007/s10734-021-00716-5

Field, K. (2020, March 26). 5 lessons from campuses that closed after natural disasters. *The Chronicle of Higher Education*. https://www.chronicle.com/article/5-lessons-from-campuses-that-closed-after-natural-disasters/

Fink, S. (1986). *Crisis management: Planning for the inevitable*. Amacom.

Fiol, C. M., & Lyles, M. A. (1985). Organizational learning. *Academy of Management Review*, 10(4), 803–813. https://doi.org/10.2307/258048

Fletcher, A., Gaines, T. L., & Loney, B. (2023, September 28). How to be a better leader amid volatility, uncertainty, complexity, and ambiguity. *Harvard Business Review*.

Fletcher, D., & Sarkar, M. (2013). Psychological resilience: A review and critique of definitions, concepts and theory. *European Psychologist*, 18(1), 12–23. http://dx.doi.org/10.1027/1016-9040/a000124

Frankl, V. E. (1992). *Man's search for meaning* (4th ed.). Beacon Press.

Frantz, J. (2012, January 9). Penn State alumni magazine takes on Jerry Sandusky scandal. *Penn Live Patriot-News*. https://www.pennlive.com/midstate/2012/01/penn_state_alumni_mag_takes_on.html

Fredrickson, B. L., Tugade, M. M., Waugh, C. E., & Larkin, G. R. (2003). What good are positive emotions in crisis? A prospective study of resilience and emotions following the terrorist attacks on the United States on September 11th, 2001. *Journal of Personality and Social Psychology*, 84(2), 365–376. https://doi.org/10.1037/0022-3514.84.2.365

Freeh Sporkin & Sullivan LLP. (2012, July 12). *Report of the Special Investigative Counsel Regarding the Actions of the Pennsylvania State University*

Related to the Child Sexual Abuse Committed by Gerald A. Sandusky.
https://www.documentcloud.org/documents/396512-report-final-071212

Fritz, C. E. (1996). *Disasters and mental health: Therapeutic principles drawn from disaster studies.* University of Delaware, Disaster Research Center. Historical and Comparative Disaster Series No. 10. http://udspace.udel .edu/handle/19716/1325 (Original work published 1961)

Fuller, R. P., Ulmer, R. R., McNatt, A., & Ruiz, J. B. (2019). Extending discourse of renewal to preparedness: Construct and scale development of readiness for renewal. *Management Communication Quarterly, 33*(2), 272–301. https://doi.org/10.1177/0893318919834333

Garvin, D. A. (1993, July–August). Building a learning organization. *Harvard Business Review, 71*(4), 78–91.

George, A., & Bennett, A. (2005). *Case studies and theory development in the social sciences.* MIT Press.

Giddens, A. (1991). *Modernity and self-identity: self and society in the late modern age.* Stanford University Press.

Gigliotti, R. A. (2016). Leader as performer; leader as human: A post-crisis discursive construction of leadership. *Atlantic Journal of Communication, 24*(4), 185–200. https://doi.org/10.1080/15456870.2016.1208660

Gigliotti, R. A. (2019). *Crisis leadership in higher education: Theory and practice.* Rutgers University Press. https://doi.org/10.36019/9781978801868

Gigliotti, R. A. (2020a). The perception of crisis, the existence of crisis: Navigating the social construction of crisis. *Journal of Applied Communication Research, 48*(5), 558–576. https://doi.org/10.1080/00909882.2020.1820553

Gigliotti, R. A. (2020b). Sudden shifts to fully online: Perceptions of campus preparedness and implications for leading through disruption. *Journal of Literacy and Technology, 21*(2), 18–36.

Gigliotti, R. A. (2021). The impact of COVID-19 on academic department chairs: Heightened complexity, accentuated liminality, and competing perceptions of reinvention. *Innovative Higher Education, 46*(1), 429–444. https://doi.org/10.1007/s10755-021-09545-x

Gigliotti, R. A. (2022a). Crisis leadership in higher education: Historical overview, organizational considerations, and implications. In *The Oxford Encyclopedia of Crisis Analysis.* Oxford University Press. https://doi.org/10.1093/acrefore/9780190228637.013.2045

Gigliotti, R. A. (2022b). Department chair perspectives on leading through prolonged and intersecting crises. *The Department Chair, 32*(3), 12–15. https://doi.org/10.1002/dch.30425

Gigliotti, R. A. (2024). Leadership generativity and the social, emotional, and pragmatic pivot from crisis to post-crisis. *Journal of Leadership Studies.* https://doi.org/10.1002/jls.21889

Gigliotti, R. A., & Dwyer, B. (2016). Cultivating dialogue: A central imperative for servant leadership. *Journal of Servant Leadership: Theory and Practice, 3*(1), 69–88.

Gigliotti, R. A., & Fortunato, J. A. (2021). Crisis leadership: A values-centered approach to crisis leadership. In B. D. Ruben, R. De Lisi, & R. A. Gigliotti, *A guide for leaders in higher education: Core concepts, competencies, and tools* (2nd ed., pp. 314–340). Stylus. https://doi.org/10.4324/9781003442769-20

Gigliotti, R. A., & Goldthwaite, C. (2021). *Leadership in academic health centers: Core concepts and critical cases.* Kendall Hunt.

Gigliotti, R. A. & O'Dowd, M. (2021). Crisis leadership in academic health centers: Principles and practices for navigating disruption. In R. A. Gigliotti & C. Goldthwaite, *Leadership in academic health centers: Core concepts and critical cases* (pp. 169–185). Kendall Hunt.

Gigliotti, R. A., Ruben, B. D., & Goldthwaite, C. (2017). *Leadership: Communication and social influence in personal and professional settings.* Kendall Hunt.

Gioia, D. A., & Chittipeddi, K. (1991). Sensemaking and sensegiving in strategic change initiation. *Strategic Management Journal, 12*(6), 433–448. https://doi.org/10.1002/smj.4250120604

Gioia, D., Thomas, J. B., Clark, S. M., & Chittipeddi, K. (1994). Symbolism and strategic change in academia: The dynamics of sensemaking and influence. *Organization Science, 5*(3), 363–383. https://doi.org/10.1287/orsc.5.3.363

Gmelch, W. H., & Miskin, V. D. (2004). *Chairing an academic department* (2nd ed.). Atwood.

Gmelch, W., & Parkay, F. (1999, April). *Becoming a department chair: Negotiating the transition from scholar to administrator* [Paper presentation]. American Educational Research Association, Montreal, Canada.

Graham, R. (2021, May 14). Meet the nun who wants you to remember you will die. *The New York Times.* https://www.nytimes.com/2021/05/14/us/memento-mori-nun.html

Grint, K. (2005). Problems, problems, problems: The social construction of leadership. *Human Relations, 58*(11), 1467–1494. https://doi.org/10.1177/0018726705061314

Gronn, P. (1983). Talk as the work: The accomplishment of school administration. *Administrative Science Quarterly, 28*(1), 1–21. https://doi.org/10.2307/2392382

Hannah, S. T., Uhl-Bien M., Avolio B. J., & Cavarretta F. L. (2009). A framework for examining leadership in extreme contexts. *Leadership Quarterly, 20*(6), 897–919. https://doi.org/10.1016/j.leaqua.2009.09.006

Hardy, C., Langley, A., Mintzberg, H., & Rose, J. (1983). Strategy formation in the university setting. *The Review of Higher Education, 6*(4), 407–433. https://doi.org/10.1353/rhe.1983.0015

Harris, A. (2018, June 5). Here's how higher education dies. *The Atlantic.* https://www.theatlantic.com/education/archive/2018/06/heres-how-higher-education-dies/561995/

Harris, T. (2007, April 16). *University shooting: At least one killed at Virginia Tech* [TV broadcast transcript], CNN. http://edition.cnn.com/TRANSCRIPTS/0704/16/ywt.01.html

Helsloot, I., Boin, A., Jacobs, B., & Comfort, L. K. (Eds.). (2012). *Mega-crises: Understanding the prospects, nature, characteristics, and the effects of cataclysmic events.* Charles C. Thomas.

Herovic E., & Veil, S. R. (2015). Some lines bring us together: Sport as crisis renewal in Bosnia-Herzegovina. *Communication, Culture & Critique, 9*(4), 517–536. https://doi.org/10.1111/cccr.12138

Hlavac, C., & Buller, J. L. (2020). Leading the academic department during the COVID-19 crisis. *The Department Chair, 31*(1), 17–19. https://doi.org/10.1002/dch.30332

Houston, J. B., & Buzzanell, P. M. (2020). Communication and resilience: Introduction to the *Journal of Applied Communication Research* special issue. *Journal of Applied Communication Research, 48*(1), 1–4. https://doi.org/10.1080/00909882.2020.1711956

Howard, M. A. (2014, October 20). *Higher education and the public good.* HuffPost. https://www.huffpost.com/entry/higher-education-and-the _b_6005080

Hu, V., & Ton-Quinlivan, V. (2021, February 24). *The reinvention of higher education.* The EvoLLLution. https://evolllution.com/revenue-streams /market_opportunities/the-reinvention-of-higher-education/

Huber, G. P. (1991). Organizational learning: The contributing processes and the literatures. *Organization Science, 2*(1), 88–115. https://doi.org/10 .1287/orsc.2.1.88

James, E. H., & Wooten, L. P. (2010). *Leading under pressure: From surviving to thriving before, during, and after a crisis.* Routledge.

James, E. H., & Wooten, L. P. (2022a, September 13). In a crisis, great leaders prioritize listening. *Harvard Business Review.* https://hbr.org /2022/09/in-a-crisis-great-leaders-prioritize-listening

James, E. H., & Wooten, L. P. (2022b). *The prepared leader: Emerge from any crisis more resilient than before.* Wharton School Press. https://doi .org/10.2307/j.ctv2n7j1qj

James, E. H., Wooten, L. P., & Dushek, K. (2011). Crisis management: Informing a new leadership research agenda. *Academy of Management Annals, 5*(1), 455–493. https://doi.org/10.1080/19416520.2011.589594

Jindal, B. (2021, March 31). A post-COVID reinvention of higher education. *The Hill.* https://thehill.com/opinion/education/545639-a-post -covid-reinvention-of-higher-education/

Johnson, J. (2012, April 27). Penn State spends millions on public relations, hires new firm. *The Washington Post.* https://www.washingtonpost.com /blogs/campus-overload/post/penn-state-spends-millions-on-public -relations-hires-new-firms/2012/04/27/gIQAAOiTIT_blog.html

Kaplan, R. S., & Norton, D. P. (2001). The strategy-focused organization. *Strategy & Leadership, 29*(3), 41–42. https://doi.org/10.1108/sl.2001 .26129cab.002

Kaye-Kauderer, H., Rodriguez, A., Levine, J., Takeguchi, Y., Machida, M., Feingold, J., Sekine, H., Katz, C., & Yanagisawa, R. (2020). Narratives of resilience in medical students following the 3/11 triple disaster: Using thematic analysis to examine paths to recovery. *Psychiatry Research, 292,* Article 113348. https://doi.org/10.1016/j.psychres.2020.113348

Kayes, D. C. (2015). *Organizational resilience: How learning sustains organizations in crisis, disaster, and breakdown.* Oxford University Press. https://doi.org/10.1093/acprof:oso/9780199791057.001.0001

Keller, G. (1983). *Academic strategy: The management revolution in American higher education.* Johns Hopkins University Press.

Kellerman, B. (2016). Leadership—It's a system, not a person! *Daedalus, 145,* 83–94. https://doi.org/10.1162/DAED_a_00399

Kent State University. (n.d.). *May 4 Memorial.* https://www.library.kent .edu/special-collections-and-archives/may-4-memorial-kent-state -university

Keohane, N. O. (2006). *Higher ground: Ethics and leadership in the modern university.* Duke University Press. https://doi.org/10.2307/j.ctv125jp6b

Knox, L. (2023). After the smoke clears, when should classes resume? *Inside Higher Ed.* https://www.insidehighered.com/news/2023/03/10 /offering-academic-flexibility-after-campus-shooting

Koehn, N. (2018). *Forged in crisis: The making of five courageous leaders.* Scribner.

Kolb, D. A. (1984). *Experiential learning: Experience as the source of learning and development.* Prentice Hall.

Koloroutis, M., & Pole, M. (2021). Trauma-informed leadership and posttraumatic growth. *Nursing Management, 52*(12), 28–34. https://doi .org/10.1097/01.NUMA.0000800336.39811.a3

Lambiase, J., & English, A. E. (2021). Passing the test: Lessons from a school district's discourse of renewal before, during, and after Hurricane Harvey. *Journal of Contingencies and Crisis Management, 29,* 36–46. https://doi.org/10.1111/1468-5973.12301

Lawrence, P. R. (1969, January). How to deal with resistance to change. *Harvard Business Review.* https://hbr.org/1969/01/how-to-deal-with -resistance-to-change

LeBas, J. (1999, November 20). Tragedy struck despite preparation. *My Aggie Nation.* https://myaggienation.com/archive/tragedy-struck-despite -preparation/article_dfd22244-e3f1-11e2-a189-0019bb2963f4.html

Ledesma, J. (2014). Conceptual frameworks and research models on resilience in leadership. *SAGE Open, 4*(3). https://doi.org/10.1177/2158244014545464

Levine, A., & Van Pelt, S. (2021). *The great upheaval: Higher education's past, present, and uncertain future.* Johns Hopkins University Press.

Levitt, B., & March, J. (1988). Organizational learning. *Annual Review of Sociology, 14*(1), 319–338. https://doi.org/10.1146/annurev.so.14.080188.001535

Lewis, L. K., & Russ, T. L. (2012). Soliciting and using input during organizational change initiatives: What are practitioners doing. *Management Communication Quarterly, 26*(2), 267–294. https://doi.org/10.1177/0893318911431804

Lewis-Strickland K. (2021). Advice from a seat at the table: Exploring the leadership resilience development of Black women university deans. *Journal of Higher Education Policy and Leadership Studies, 2*(1), 29–43. https://doi.org/10.52547/johepal.2.1.29

Llopis, G. (2020, October 17). Post pandemic: How must colleges and universities reinvent themselves? *Forbes.* https://www.forbes.com/sites/glennllopis/2020/10/17/post-pandemic-how-must-colleges-and-universities-reinvent-themselves/?sh=3361b3aa3e88

Lundqvist, D., Wallo, A., Coetzer, A., & Kock, H. (2023). Leadership and learning at work: A systematic literature review of learning-oriented leadership. *Journal of Leadership & Organizational Studies, 30*(2), 205–238. https://doi.org/10.1177/15480518221133970

Maitlis, S., & Lawrence, T. B. (2007). Triggers and enablers of sensegiving in organizations. *Academy of Management Journal, 50*(1), 57–84. https://doi.org/10.5465/amj.2007.24160971

Maitlis, S., & Sonenshein, S. (2010), Sensemaking in crisis and change: Inspiration and insights from Weick (1988). *Journal of Management Studies, 47*(3), 551–580. https://doi.org/10.1111/j.1467-6486.2010.00908.x

Mancini, A. D., Littleton, H. L., & Grills, A. E. (2016). Can people benefit from acute stress? Social support, psychological improvement, and resilience after the Virginia Tech campus shootings. *Clinical Psychological Science, 4*(3), 401–417. https://doi.org/10.1177/2167702615601001

Masten A. S. (2014). Global perspectives on resilience in children and youth. *Child Development, 85*(1), 6–20. https://doi.org/10.1111/cdev.12205

McClure, K. R., & Fryar, A. H. (2022). The great faculty disengagement. *The Chronicle of Higher Education.* https://www.chronicle.com/article /the-great-faculty-disengagement

McKenzie, L. (2021, February 14). UMGC at a "pivotal moment." *Inside Higher Ed.* https://www.insidehighered.com/news/2021/02/15/new -university-maryland-global-campus-president-takes-over-online -universities-are

McNamara, A. (2021). Crisis management in higher education in the time of COVID-19: The case of actor training. *Education Sciences, 11*(3), Article 132. https://doi.org/10.3390/educsci11030132

Microsoft. (2021, March 22). *2021 Work Trend Index: Annual report: The next great disruption is hybrid work—are we ready?* https://www.microsoft .com/en-us/worklab/work-trend-index/hybrid-work

Miller, M. T. (2020). Do learning organizations learn? Higher education institutions and pandemic response strategies. *Learning Organization, 28*(1), 84–93. https://doi.org/10.1108/TLO-09-2020-0159

Milner, R. J., & Echterling, L. G. (2021). Co-constructing meaning in the time of coronavirus. *Journal of Constructivist Psychology, 34*(3), 295–308. https://doi.org/10.1080/10720537.2020.1864691

Mintz, B. (2021). Neoliberalism and the crisis in higher education: The cost of ideology. *American Journal of Economics and Sociology, 80*(1), 79–112. https://doi.org/10.1111/ajes.12370

Mintzberg, H. (1979). *The structuring of organizations.* Prentice Hall.

Mintzberg, H. (1987). The strategy concept I: Five Ps for strategy. *California Management Review, 30*(1), 11–24. https://doi.org/10.2307/41165263

Miron, L. R., Orcutt, H. K., & Kumpula, M. J. (2014). Differential predictors of transient stress versus posttraumatic stress disorder: Evaluating risk following targeted mass violence. *Behavior Therapy, 45*(6), 791–805. https://doi.org/10.1016/j.beth.2014.07.005

Mitroff, I. (2004). *Crisis leadership: Planning for the unthinkable.* Wiley.

Mooallem, J., & Gilbertson, A. (2023, February 22). What happened to us. *The New York Times Magazine.* https://www.nytimes.com/interactive /2023/02/22/magazine/covid-pandemic-oral-history.html

Morrison, T. (2007). *Beloved.* Vintage Classics.

Morse, J. (1999, November 29). A good time goes bad. *Time.*

Mosser, M. (2023, July 27). *Half of your employees are looking to leave.* Gallup. https://www.gallup.com/workplace/506819/half-employees-looking-leave.aspx

Moynihan, D. P. (2008). From intercrisis to intracrisis learning. *Journal of Contingencies and Crisis Management, 17*(3), 189–198. https://doi.org/10.1111/j.1468-5973.2009.00579.x

Murphy, P. (1996). Chaos theory as a model for managing issues and crises. *Public Relations Review, 22*(2), 95–113. https://doi.org/10.1016/S0363-8111(96)90001-6

Nandy, M., Lodh, S., & Tang, A. (2021). Lessons from COVID-19 and a resilience model for higher education. *Industry and Higher Education, 35*(1), 3–9. https://doi.org/10.1177/0950422220962696

Nathan, M. L., & Kovoor-Misra, S. (2002). No pain, yet gain: Vicarious organizational learning from crises in an inter-organizational field. *Journal of Applied Behavioral Science, 38*(2), 245–266. https://doi.org/10.1177/0028630203 8002006

Nucifora, F., Langlieb, A., Siegal, E., Everly, G., & Kaminsky, M. (2007). Building resistance, resilience, and recovery in the wake of school and workplace violence. *Disaster Medicine and Public Health Preparedness, 1*(Suppl. 1), S33–S37. https://doi.org/10.1097/DMP.0b013e31814b98ae

Örtenblad, A., & Koris, R. (2014). Is the learning organization idea relevant to higher educational institutions? A literature review and a "multi-stakeholder contingency approach." *International Journal of Educational Management, 28*(2), 173–214. https://doi.org/10.1108/IJEM-01-2013-0010

Osterman, K. F. (1990). Reflective practice: A new agenda for education. *Education and Urban Society, 22*(2), 133–152. https://doi.org/10.1177/001312459022002002

Oxford University Press. (n.d.). Reinvention. In *Oxford English dictionary.* Retrieved July 26, 2020, from https://www.oed.com/search/dictionary/?scope=Entries&q=reinvention

Paquette, G. (2021, March 4). Can higher education save itself? *The Chronicle of Higher Education.* https://www.chronicle.com/article/can-higher-ed-save-itself?sra=true&cid=gen_sign_in

Pauchant, T., & Mitroff, I. (1992). *Transforming the crisis prone organization.* Jossey-Bass.

Pearce, W. B., & Cronen, V. E. (1980). *Communication, action, and meaning: The creation of social realities.* Praeger.

Pearson, C. M., & Clair, J. A. (1998). Reframing crisis management. *Academy of Management Review, 23*(1), 59–76. https://doi.org/10.2307/259099

Peiritsch, A. R. (2019). Starbucks' racial-bias crisis: Toward a rhetoric of renewal. *Journal of Media Ethics, 34*(4), 215–227. https://doi.org/10.1080/23736992.2019.1673757

Perrow, C. (1984). *Normal accidents: Living with high-risk technologies.* Princeton University Press.

Perry, R., & Quarantelli, E. (Eds.). (2005). *What is a disaster? New answers to old questions.* Xlibris. https://doi.org/10.4324/9780203984833

Pew Research Center. (2021). *What makes life meaningful? Views from 17 advanced economies.* https://www.pewresearch.org/global/2021/11/18/what-makes-life-meaningful-views-from-17-advanced-economies/

Piaget, J. (1936). *Origins of intelligence in the child.* Routledge & Kegan Paul.

Pillay-Naidoo, D., & Nel, P. (2022). Testing a model of resilience for women leaders: A strengths based approach. *Australian Journal of Psychology, 74*(1), Article 2138542. https://doi.org/10.1080/00049530.2022.2138542

Pondy, L. R. (1978). Leadership is a language game. In M. W. McCall & M. M. Lombardo (Eds.), *Leadership: Where else can we go?* Duke University Press.

Porac, J. F. (2002). *Organizing for resilience: Discussant comments* [Paper presentation]. Annual Meeting of the Academy of Management, Denver, CO.

Pyle, A. S., Fuller, R. P., & Ulmer, R. R. (2020). Discourse of renewal: State of the discipline and a vision for the future. In H. D. O'Hair & M. J. O'Hair (Eds.), *The handbook of applied communication research* (pp. 343–361). Wiley-Blackwell. https://doi.org/10.1002/9781119399926.ch21

Quarantelli, E. (Ed.). (1998). *What is a disaster?* Routledge.

Ramirez, Q. (2019, July 5). *Texas A&M's century-old bonfire tradition evolves in wake of deadly collapse.* Fox San Antonio. https://foxsanantonio.com/texas-ams-century-old-bonfire-tradition-evolves-in-wake-of-deadly-collapse

Ramos, C., & Leal, I. (2012). Posttraumatic growth in the aftermath of trauma: A literature review about related factors and application contexts. *Psychology, Community & Health, 2*(1), 43–54. https://doi.org /10.23668/psycharchives.2243

Reese, S. (2017). Is the higher education institution a learning organization (or can it become one)? *Learning Organization, 24*(5), 378–380. https:// doi.org/10.1108/TLO-05-2017-0041

Renesch, J., & Chawla, S. (2006). *Learning organizations: Developing cultures for tomorrow's workplace.* Routledge.

Rhoden, G., & Paul, D. (2022, February 2). *73 Confederate monuments were removed or renamed last year, report finds.* ABC News. https://abc17news .com/news/national-world/cnn-national/2022/02/02/73-confederate -monuments-were-removed-or-renamed-last-year-report-finds/

Richardson G. E. (2002). The metatheory of resilience and resiliency. *Journal of Clinical Psychology, 58*(3), 307–321. https://doi.org/10.1002/jclp.10020

Rider, E. A., Kurtz, S., Slade, D., Longmaid, H. E., Ho, M., Pun, J. K., Eggins, S., & Branch, W. T. (2014). The International Charter for Human Values in Healthcare: An interprofessional global collaboration to enhance values and communication in healthcare. *Patient Education and Counseling, 96*(3), 273–280. https://doi.org/10.1016/j.pec .2014.06.017

Rosenberg, B. (2023, September 25). Higher Ed's ruinous resistance to change. *The Chronicle of Higher Education.* https://www.chronicle.com /article/higher-eds-ruinous-resistance-to-change

Rosowsky, D. (2020, September 5). Where does higher education go next? *Forbes.*

Ruben, B. D. (2011). *Understanding, planning, and leading organizational change.* National Association of College and University Business Officers.

Ruben, B. D. (2020). *Guidance for college and university planning for a post-COVID-19 world* [White paper]. Stylus.

Ruben, B. D., De Lisi, R., & Gigliotti, R. A. (2021). *A guide for leaders in higher education: Core concepts, competencies, and tools* (2nd ed.). Stylus.

Ruben, B. D. & Gigliotti, R. A. (2016). Leadership as social influence: An expanded view of leadership communication theory and practice.

Journal of Leadership and Organizational Studies, 23(4), 467–479. https://doi.org/10.1177/1548051816641876

Ruben, B. D. & Gigliotti, R. A. (2017). Communication: Sine qua non of organizational leadership theory and practice. *International Journal of Business Communication, 54*(1), 12–30. https://doi.org/10.1177/2329488416675447

Ruben, B. D., & Gigliotti, R. A. (2019). *Leadership, communication, and social influence: A theory of resonance, activation, and cultivation.* Emerald. https://doi.org/10.1108/9781838671181

Ruben, B. D., & Gigliotti, R. A. (2021). Explaining incongruities between leadership theory and practice: Integrating theories of resonance, communication, and systems. *Leadership & Organization Development Journal, 42*(6), 942–957. https://doi.org/10.1108/LODJ-02-2021-0072

Rumelt, R. P. (2011). *Good strategy bad strategy: The difference and why it matters.* Currency. https://doi.org/10.1108/sd.2012.05628haa.002

Rutgers University. (n.d.). *Institute for the Study of Global Racial Justice.* https://globalracialjustice.rutgers.edu/

Saltmarsh, S. (2011). Economic subjectivities in higher education: Self, policy and practice in the knowledge economy. *Cultural Studies Review, 17*(2), 115–139. https://doi.org/10.5130/csr.v17i2.2007

Sanchez, M., Lamont, M., & Zilberstein, S. (2022). How American college students understand social resilience and navigate towards the future during Covid and the movement for racial justice. *Social Science & Medicine, 301,* Article 114890. https://doi.org/10.1016/j.socscimed.2022.114890

Santiago, D., Labandera, E., & Arroyo, C. (2023, February). Institutional resilience in Puerto Rico: A first look at efforts by Puerto Rican HSIs. *Excelencia in Education.*

Schön, D. A. (1987). *Educating the reflective practitioner: Toward a new design for teaching and learning in the professions.* Jossey-Bass.

School Crisis Recovery & Renewal Project. (n.d.). *About us.* https://schoolcrisishealing.org/about-us/

Schroeder, R. (2021, February 17). Time for reinvention, not just replication or revision. *Inside Higher Ed.* https://www.insidehighered.com/blogs/online-trending-now/time-reinvention-not-just-replication-or-revision

Schwandt, D., & Marquadt, M. J. (2000). *Organizational learning: From world-class theories to global best practices.* Routledge.

Seeger, M. W. (2006). Best practices in crisis communication: An expert panel process. *Journal of Applied Communication Research, 34*(3), 232–244. https://doi.org/10.1080/00909880600769944

Seeger, M. W. (2018). Answering the call for scholarship: The *Journal of International Crisis and Risk Communication Research. Journal of International Crisis and Risk Communication Research, 1*(1), 7–10. https://doi.org /10.30658/jicrcr.1.1.1

Seeger, M. W., Nowling, W., & Seeger, H. S. (2024). Keystone theories of postcrisis discourse: Communication Theory of Resilience and Discourse of Renewal. *Journal of Contingencies and Crisis Management, 32*, e12533. https://doi.org/10.1111/1468-5973.12533

Seeger, M. W., & Padgett, D. R. G. (2010). From image restoration to renewal: Approaches to understanding postcrisis communication. *Review of Communication, 10*(2), 127–141. https://doi.org/10.1080/15358590903545263

Seeger, M. W., & Sellnow, T. L. (2016). *Narratives of crisis: Telling stories of ruin and renewal.* Stanford University Press.

Seeger, M. W., Sellnow, T. L., & Ulmer, R. R. (2003). *Communication and organizational crisis.* Praeger.

Seeger, M. W., & Ulmer, R. R. (2001). Virtuous responses to organizational crisis: Aaron Feuerstein and Milt Cole. *Journal of Business Ethics, 31*(4), 369–376. https://doi.org/10.1023/A:1010759319845

Seeger, M. W., & Ulmer, R. R. (2002). A post-crisis discourse of renewal: The cases of Malden Mills and Cole Hardwoods. *Journal of Applied Communication Research, 30*(2), 126–142. https://doi.org/10.1080 /00909880216578

Selingo, J. (2022). *Reimagining the university: Beyond the return to normal in the decade ahead.* Academic Intelligence and Kaplan. https://kaplan .com/universities/reimagining-the-university-white-paper

Sellnow, D. D., Iverson, J., & Sellnow, T. L. (2017). The evolution of the operational earthquake forecasting community of practice: The L'Aquila communication crisis as a triggering event for organizational renewal. *Journal of Applied Communication Research, 45*(2), 121–139. https://doi.org /10.1080/00909882.2017.1288295

Sellnow, T. L., & Seeger, M. W. (2020). *Theorizing crisis communication* (2nd ed.). Wiley.

Senge, P. M. (2006). *The fifth discipline: The art and practice of the learning organization.* Doubleday.

Shaya, N., Abukhait, R., Madani, R., & Khattak, M. N. (2022). Organizational resilience of higher education institutions: An empirical study during COVID-19 pandemic. *Higher Education Policy.* https://doi.org /10.1057/s41307-022-00272-2

Silver, R. C., Holman, E. A., & Garfin, D. R. (2021). Coping with cascading collective traumas in the United States. *Nature Human Behavior, 5,* 4–6. https://doi.org/10.1038/s41562-020-00981-x

Slagle, D. R., Chatham-Carpenter, A., & Williams, A. M. (2022). A discourse of renewal: Higher education leadership and crisis communication during Black Lives Matter. *Public Integrity.* https://doi.org/10 .1080/10999922.2022.2068320

Slovic, P., & Västfjäll, D. (2015). The more who die, the less we care: Psychic numbing and genocide. In S. Kaul & D. Kim (Eds.), *Imagining human rights* (pp. 55–68). De Gruyter. https://doi.org/10.1515 /9783110376616-005

Smith, D., & Elliott, D. (2007). Exploring the barriers to learning from crisis: Organizational learning and crisis. *Management Learning, 38*(5), 519–538. https://doi.org/10.1177/1350507607083205

Smith, J. S. (2018). From the "Ayotte Evasion" to rejecting Trump: Senator Kelly Ayotte's post-crisis discourse of renewal. *Communication Quarterly, 66*(2), 117–137. https://doi.org/10.1080/01463373.2018.1438487

Smith, M. D. (2023, October 5). The public is giving up on higher ed. *Chronicle of Higher Education.* https://www.chronicle.com/article/the -public-is-giving-up-on-higher-ed

Snook, S. A. (2000). *Friendly fire: The accidental shootdown of U.S. Black Hawks over Northern Iraq.* Princeton University Press. https://doi.org /10.1515/9781400840977

Solnit, R. (2010). *A paradise built in hell: The extraordinary communities that arise in disaster.* Penguin.

Sommer, S. A., Howell, J. M., & Hadley, C. N. (2016). Keeping positive and building strength: The role of affect and team leadership in

developing resilience during an organizational crisis. *Group &
Organization Management, 41*(2), 172–202. https://doi.org/10.1177
/1059601115578027

Spears, L. C. (2002). Introduction: Tracing the past, present, and future
of servant leadership. In L. Spears & M. Lawrence (Eds.), *Focus on
leadership: Servant leadership for the twenty-first century* (pp. 1–16). Wiley.

Spector, B. (2019). *Constructing crisis: Leaders, crises and claims of urgency.*
Cambridge University Press. https://doi.org/10.1017/9781108551663

Spector, B. (2020). Even in a global pandemic, there's no such thing as a
crisis. *Leadership, 16*(3), 303–313. https://doi.org/10.1177/1742715020927111

Steger, C. W. (2007, May). Convocation remarks. *Virginia Tech Magazine.*
https://www.archive.vtmag.vt.edu/memorial07/convocation.html

Stephens, K. K., Jahn, J. L. S., Fox, S., Charoensap-Kelly, P., Mitra, R.,
Sutton, J., Waters, E. D., Xie, B., & Meisenbach, R. J. (2020).
Collective sensemaking around COVID-19: Experiences, concerns,
and agendas for our rapidly changing organizational lives. *Management
Communication Quarterly, 34*(3), 426–457. https://doi.org/10.1177
/0893318920934890

Stern, E. K. (2009). Crisis navigation: Lessons from history for the crisis
manager in chief. *Governance: An International Journal of Policy,
Administration, and Institutions, 22*(2), 189–202. https://doi.org/10.1111/j
.1468-0491.2009.01431.x

Stern, E., Deverell, E., Fors, F., & Newlove-Eriksson, L. (2014). Post
mortem crisis analysis: Dissecting the London bombings of July 2005.
Journal of Organizational Effectiveness: People and Performance, 1(4),
402–422. https://doi.org/10.1108/JOEPP-09-2014-0058

Sutcliffe, K. M., & Vogus, T. J. (2003). Organizing for resilience. In K. S.
Cameron, J. E. Dutton, & R. E. Quinn (Eds.), *Positive organizational
scholarship: Foundations of a new discipline* (pp. 94–110). Berrett-Koehler.

Sutin, S. E., & Jacob, W. J. (2016). *Strategic transformation of higher
education: Challenges and solutions in a global economy.* Rowman and
Littlefield.

Taylor, A. (2020, September 8). The end of the university. *New Republic.*
https://newrepublic.com/article/159233/coronavirus-pandemic-collapse
-college-universities

Tedeschi, R. G., & Calhoun, L. G. (1995). *Trauma and transformation: Growing in the aftermath of suffering.* Sage. https://doi.org/10.4135/9781483326931

Tedeschi, R. G., Cann, A., Taku, K., Senol-Durak, E., & Calhoun, L. G. (2017). The posttraumatic growth inventory: A revision integrating existential and spiritual change. *Journal of Traumatic Stress, 30*(1), 11–18. https://doi.org/10.1002/jts.22155

Tedeschi, R. G., Shakespeare-Finch, J., Taku, K., & Calhoun, L. G. (2018). *Posttraumatic growth: Theory, research, and applications.* Routledge. https://doi.org/10.4324/9781315527451

Texas A&M University. (n.d.). *Bonfire Memorial.* https://bonfire.tamu.edu/

Thayer, L. (1988). Leadership/communication: A critical review and a modest proposal. In G. M. Goldhaber & G. A. Barnett (Eds.), *Handbook of organizational communication* (pp. 231–263). Ablex.

Thelin, J. R. (2019). *A history of American higher education* (3rd ed.). Johns Hopkins University Press. https://doi.org/10.56021/9781421428826

Thirty-Third Statewide Investigating Grand Jury. (2022). *Grand jury report on alleged Penn State sex abuse.* https://www.documentcloud.org/documents/264894-sandusky-grand-jury-presentment

Thompson, B., Jerome, A. M., Payne, H. J., Mazer, J. P., Kirby, E. G., & Pfohl, W. (2017). Analyzing postcrisis challenges and strategies associated with school shootings: An application of discourse of renewal theory. *Communication Studies, 68*(5), 533–551. https://doi.org/10.1080/10510974.2017.1373370

Toft, B., & Reynolds, S. (1997). *Learning from disasters.* Palgrave Macmillan.

Tromp, S., & Ruben, B. D. (2021). Strategic planning: Translating aspirations into realities. In B. D. Ruben, R. De Lisi, & R. A. Gigliotti, *A guide for leaders in higher education: Core concepts, competencies, and tools* (2nd ed., pp. 245–264). Stylus.

Turner, B. A. (1976). The organizational and interorganizational development of disasters. *Administrative Science Quarterly, 21*(3), 378–397. https://doi.org/10.2307/2391850

Ulmer, R. R. (2001). Effective crisis management through established stakeholder relationships: Malden Mills as a case study. *Management*

Communication Quarterly, 14(4), 590–615. https://doi.org/10.1177
/0893318901144003

Ulmer, R. R., & Pyle, A. S. (2021). Finding renewal in the midst of
disaster: The case of the Deepwater Horizon oil spill. *Public Relations
Review, 47*(1), 1–12. https://doi.org/10.1016/j.pubrev.2020.102001

Ulmer, R. R., Seeger, M. W., & Sellnow, T. L. (2007). Post-crisis communication and renewal: Expanding the parameters of post-crisis discourse.
Public Relations Review, 33(2), 130–134. https://doi.org/10.1016/j.pubrev
.2006.11.015.

Ulmer, R. R., & Sellnow, T. L. (2002). Crisis management and the discourse
of renewal: Understanding the potential for positive outcomes of crisis.
Public Relations Review, 28, 361–365. https://doi.org/10.1016/S0363
-8111(02)00165-0

Ulmer, R. R., Sellnow, T. L., & Seeger, M. W. (2009). Post-crisis
communication and renewal: Understanding the potential for positive
outcomes in crisis communication. In R. L. Heath and D. H. O'Hair
(Eds.), *Handbook of Risk and Crisis Communication* (pp. 302–322).
Routledge.

Ulmer R. R., Sellnow T. L., & Seeger M. W. (2019). *Effective crisis
communication: Moving from crisis to opportunity* (4th ed.). Sage.

Ulmer R. R., Sellnow T. L., & Seeger M. W. (2022). *Effective crisis
communication: Moving from crisis to opportunity* (5th ed.). Sage.

University of British Columbia. (n.d.). *The Okanagan Charter.* https://
wellbeing.ubc.ca/okanagan-charter

U.S. Bureau of Labor Statistics. (2022, July). The "Great Resignation" in
perspective. *Monthly Labor Review.* https://www.bls.gov/opub/mlr
/2022/article/the-great-resignation-in-perspective.htm

U.S. Fire Administration. (1999). *Bonfire collapse: Texas A&M University.*
USFA-TR-133. Homeland Security. https://web.archive.org/web
/20170216013653/https://www.usfa.fema.gov/downloads/pdf
/publications/tr-133.pdf

Veil, S. R., Sellnow, T. L., & Heald, M. (2011). Memorializing crisis: The
Oklahoma City National Memorial as renewal discourse. *Journal of
Applied Communication Research, 39*(2), 164–183. https://doi.org/10.1080
/00909882.2011.557390

Veil, S. R., Woods, C. L., & Crace, R. (2021). Crisis memorials: Balancing renewal and resilience. In *Oxford Research Encyclopedia*. Oxford University Press. https://doi.org/10.1093/acrefore/9780190228637.013.1970

Viera, M. (2011, November 9). Paterno is finished at Penn State, and president is out. *The New York Times*. https://www.nytimes.com/2011/11/10/sports/ncaafootball/-joe-paterno-and-graham-spanier-out-at-penn-state.html

Virginia Tech. (n.d.). *April 16 Memorial*. https://www.weremember.vt.edu/april-16-memorial.html

Virginia Tech Review Panel. (2007, August). *Mass shootings at Virginia Tech, April 16, 2007*. https://scholar.lib.vt.edu/prevail/docs/VTReviewPanelReport.pdf

Vogus, T. J., & Sutcliffe, K. M. (2007). Organizational resilience: Towards a theory and research agenda. In *2007 IEEE International Conference on Systems, Man and Cybernetics* (pp. 3418–3422). IEEE. https://doi.org/10.1109/ICSMC.2007.4414160

Vygotsky, L. S. (1978). *Mind in society: The development of higher psychological processes*. Harvard University Press.

Wagnild, G. M., & Young, H. M. (1993). Development and psychometric evaluation of the resilience scale. *Journal of Nursing Measurement, 1*(2), 165–178.

Walsh, F. (2007). Traumatic loss and major disasters: Strengthening family and community resilience. *Family Process, 46*(2), 207–227. https://doi.org/10.1111/j.1545-5300.2007.00205.x

Walsh, F., & McGoldrick, M. (2004). Loss and the family: A systemic perspective. In F. Walsh & M. McGoldrick (Eds.), *Living beyond loss: Death in the family* (pp. 3–26). Norton.

Waterman, R. H. (1990). *Adhocracy: The power to change*. Whittle Direct Books.

Weick, K. E. (1979). *The social psychology of organizing*. Addison-Wesley.

Weick, K. E. (1988). Enacted sense-making in crisis situations. *Journal of Management Studies, 25*(4), 305–317. https://doi.org/10.1111/j.1467-6486.1988.tb00039.x

Weick, K. E. (1993). The collapse of sensemaking in organizations: The Mann Gulch disaster. *Administrative Science Quarterly, 38*(4), 628–652. https://doi.org/10.2307/2393339

Weick, K. E. (1995). *Sensemaking in organizations*. Sage.

Weick, K. E., & Sutcliffe, K. M. (2001). *Managing the unexpected: Assuring high performance in an age of complexity*. Jossey-Bass.

Weick, K. E., Sutcliffe, K. M., & Obstfeld, D. (1999). Organizing for high reliability: Processes of collective mindfulness. In R. I. Sutton & B. M. Staw (Eds.), *Research in Organizational Behavior* (pp. 81–123). Elsevier Science/JAI Press.

White, J., & Weathersby, R. (2005). Can universities become true learning organizations? *Learning Organization, 12*(3), 292–298. https://doi.org/10.1108/09696470510592539

Whitford, E. (2021, August 4). Going beyond the rhetoric. *Inside Higher Ed.* https://www.insidehighered.com/news/2021/08/05/naspa-report-examines-statements-wake-george-floyds-murder

Wilson, R. C., Crenshaw, J. T., & Yoder-Wise, P. S. (2022). Call to action: Prioritizing reflective practices for leadership success. *Nurse Leader, 20*(3), 258–264. https://doi.org/10.1016/j.mnl.2022.01.008

Wilson, S. R., Kuang, K., Hintz, E. A., & Buzzanell, P. M. (2021). Developing and validating the communication resilience processes scale. *Journal of Communication, 71*(3), 478–513. https://doi.org/10.1093/joc/jqab013

Winn, Z. (2017, April 13). The Virginia Tech shooting's impact on emergency preparedness. *Campus Safety*. https://www.campussafetymagazine.com/clery/virginia_tech_shooting_anniversary_emergency_preparedness/

Wombacher, K., Herovic, E., Sellnow, T. L., & Seeger, M. W. (2018). The complexities of place in crisis renewal discourse: A case study of the Sandy Hook Elementary School shooting. *Journal of Contingencies and Crisis Management, 26*(1), 164–172. https://doi.org/10.1111/1468-5973.12186

Wooten, L. P., & James, E. H. (2004). When firms fail to learn: The perpetuation of discrimination in the workplace. *Journal of Management Inquiry, 13*(1), 23–33. https://doi.org/10.1177/1056492603259059

Xu, S. (2018). Discourse of renewal: Developing multiple-item measurement and analyzing effects on relationships. *Public Relations Review, 44*(1), 108–119. https://doi.org/10.1016/j.pubrev.2017.09.005

Index

chaos theory, 85, 112–113
Chapin, Ethan, 121
Chawla, S., 23
child abuse scandal, 50–57
Cho, Seung-Hui, 28, 29
chronic crisis (institutional crisis), 6
Chronicle of Higher Education, 86
clarity in crisis leadership, 107
Clery Act, 30
climate-related disasters, 38
CNF model. *See* crisis navigation
    framework model
College and University Professional
    Association for Human Resources,
    xii
Columbia University, 74
communication theory of resilience
    (CTR), 40, *41–42*, 42–43, 47–48
communicative process: collapse in,
    29–30; COVID-19 leadership,
    75–79; crisis management and
    crisis leadership, 14; dialogue
    and renewal, 107–111, 121; dis-
    course of renewal, 111–117; effi-
    ciency (factor in post-crisis
    communication), 115; elements of,
    107–108, *108*; factors in post-crisis
    communication, 115; fundamental
    role, 7, 13, 16; importance during
    post-crisis, 9; indicators of, 115–
    116; meaning-making in, 66,
    68–70, 71; scales to measure, 115.
    See also framing of crisis; sense-
    giving; sensemaking
compassion, 119
Confederate memorials, 123–124
consistency, demonstrating, 7, 13, 107
Constructing Crisis (Spector), 4
contingency theories of leadership, 70
Coombs, W. T., 6
coping, process of. *See* resilience
    (leadership practice)
core values (health-care interaction), 10
Coulson, H., 48

COVID-19 pandemic: change in labor
    market, xi–xii, 2–4; financial
    impact, 92; as institutional crisis,
    6, 38; leadership challenges, 75–79,
    89–90; manifestations of resil-
    ience, 49; meaning-making in,
    71–72, 73–79; mental health issues,
    83, 84, 89–90, 91, 93; ontological
    insecurity, 74–75; periods within,
    7–8; post-COVID VS. pre-
    COVID, 86; pursuing reinven-
    tion, 83, 84, 86–88, 92; racial,
    socioeconomic, geographic dis-
    parities, 74; uncertainty surround-
    ing, 12; views of post-crisis
    reinvention, 89–94
creator (sensemaking role), 68, 79
Crenshaw, J. T., 45
crisis: after-action review, 17; ambigu-
    ous nature, 72–73; clusters, 6;
    contemporary conditions, 1–9;
    cosmology episode, 61; defined, 1,
    4–6; described, 1–2, 106–107;
    disruption of core mission/pur-
    pose/existence, 10; effects of
    trauma, 44; emergency prepared-
    ness, 29–30; enacted vs. encoun-
    tered, 67; life cycle, 7–8; models
    for guidance, 12–13; as opportuni-
    ties, 72–73, 85; organization's
    character exposed, 116; phase of
    crisis, 7; process of defining/
    labeling/responding, 7, 11–15; as
    threats, 72–73; transition to post-
    crisis, xiii; triaging needs, 7; types,
    5–7; warning signs, 27–29. *See also*
    higher education; post-crisis
    leadership
crisis aftermath. *See* post-crisis
crisis communication. *See* communica-
    tive process
crisis leadership: advancing renewal,
    107–111; crisis management vs., 13,
    107; elements of communication,

James, E. H., 31–32, 34, 35, 72
Johnson & Johnson, 6

Kaplan, R. S., 95
Keller, G., 96
Kent State University, 124
Keohane, Nannerl, 24, 88
Kernodle, Xana, 121
Kiefer, Anselm, 84–85
Knox, L., 121–122
Kolb, D. A., 19
Koloroutis, M., 119
Koris, R., 23, 24
Kuang, K., 40

Lawrence, P. R., 96
leadership. *See* crisis leadership; post-crisis leadership
Leal, I., 45
learning (leadership practice): in aftermath of crisis, 25–31, 72; balancing emergence and emergency, 21; barriers to effective learning, 25–26; collective learning, 17; developing reactive capabilities, 26; encouraging, xiv, 15, 17–18, 34–35; experiential learning, 19–20, 35; focusing upon one set of threats, 26–27; higher education applications, 21–25; integration of experience and reflection, 19; *learning as crisis*, 26–27, 30–31; *learning for crisis*, 26, 30, 31; *learning from crisis*, 27, 30, 31; *learning in crisis mode*, 20–21; organization learning process, 18–21; post-crisis leadership action, 31–35; process-tracing approach, 32–34; promotion of, 14; resistance to, 26; role of leaders, 23–24; theory, 19; in times of crisis, 18–21; types of, 30–31. *See also* listening, meaningful
learning organization: described, 21–24; mental models, 22; obstacles

to becoming, 24; personal mastery, 22; shared vision, 22; team learning, 22; types of, 23. *See also* higher education; systems thinking
LeBas, J., 27
Levine, A., 3
Lewis, L. K., 98
life, loss of. *See* death
listening, meaningful, 31–33, 109, 1221
logotherapy, psychological theory of, 64
London bombings, 33

Maitlis, S., 67
manufacturer recall crises, 115
mass shooting, 6, 18, 28–31, 38, 48, 113–115, 121–122, 124
mass violence, 48
McNatt, A., 115
meaning-making (leadership practice): communicative process: 62, 66, 68–70, 71, 75–79; conditions, 62–63; in COVID-19 pandemic, 71–72, 73–79; factors associated with meaningful life, 64, 65; framing and management of meaning, 66, 71–73, 76–79; higher education applications, 73–79; importance during post-crisis, 9; intersection of leaders, followers, situation, 70; pathways of discovery, 64; post-crisis leadership action, 66–70, 79–81; search for meaning, 62–66; sensemaking and sensegiving, 66–70; stimulating, xiv, 15, 61–62, 71–72
Mellon Foundation, Andrew W., 123
memento mori, 64–66
memorials and renewal, 115, 122–124
memory, collective, 123
Méndez, A. L., 111
mental health issues, 6. *See also* COVID-19 pandemic: mental health issues

COVID-19 pandemic; crisis leadership; learning (leadership practice); higher education; meaning-making (leadership practice); post-crisis; reinvention (leadership practice); renewal (leadership practice); resilience (leadership practice)
pre-crisis (phase of crisis), 7
presence, demonstrating, 7, 107
preventable cluster crisis, 6
prevention management, 107
privacy laws, 29
process-tracing approach: chronology/narrative, 33; contextualization, 33; decision occasions, 33; described, 32–33; questions to structure after-action review, 34; steps for adapted version, 33–34; thematic comparison, 33
prospective focus (factor in post-crisis communication), 115
psychic numbing, 38
Puerto Rico and resilience strategies, 49–50
Purdue University, 78–79

racial unrest, 48, 76–77, 105–106, 115, 121, 122–123
racism, 122–123. *See also* racial unrest
Ramos, C., 45
recovery (phase of crisis), xiii, 124–125
reflection: importance during post-crisis, 9, 18–20, 81; reflection-for-action, 19; reflection-in-action, 19; reflection-on-action, 19; types of, 19–20
reimagination. *See* reinvention (leadership practice): reimagination
reinvention (leadership practice): competing views of, 89–94; defined, 84–84; education strategy, 83–84; 94–97; higher importance during post-crisis, 9, 89, 92; individual

and collective opportunities, 4, 84, 85; input solicitation, 98–99; key areas for innovation, 101–103, 102; leadership action, 90–94, 101–103; promise and pitfalls, 85–89; pursuing, xiv, 15, 83–85; reaction to change, 97–98; reimagination, 83, 89; resistance, 85, 97–101; transformation, 83, 84, 85, 89; value of, 101
remote education. *See* higher education: online operations
Renesch, J., 23
renewal (leadership practice): advancing, xiv, 15, 105–107, 120–124; characteristics, 112; cultivating, xiv; dialogue of renewal theory, 111; discourse of renewal, 111–117, 121; healing and optimism, 115, 119, 120–123; higher education applications, 120–124; humanity, dialogue, ethic of care, 107–111; importance during post-crisis, 9, 125; individual and collective transformation, 124–126; memorials and renewal, 115, 122–124; as moral imperative, 114; narratives, 113; organizational readiness, 115–116, 116; people-centered leadership, 106–107; post-crisis leadership action, 116–117, 124–126; relational practices, 119–120, 120; scales to measure communication, 115; systems approach, 118; trauma-informed leadership, 106, 117–120
reputation-driven response, 11–12, 107
research misconduct, 6
resilience (leadership practice): aftermath of Sandusky scandal, 50–57; changes from trauma, 44–45, 47, 46; collective resilience, 43, 47, 49; communication theory of resilience (CTR), 40, 41–42, 42–43, 47–48; cultivating, xiv, 37–39;

About the Author

RALPH A. GIGLIOTTI, PHD, serves as assistant vice president for organizational leadership in University Academic Affairs at Rutgers University. He also holds part-time faculty appointments in the Department of Communication (School of Communication and Information), PhD Program in Higher Education (Graduate School of Education), Department of Family Medicine and Community Health (Robert Wood Johnson Medical School), and Rutgers Business School. His research and consulting interests explore topics related to leadership, crisis, strategy, team dynamics, organizational communication, and training and development within the context of higher education. He is the author of *Crisis Leadership in Higher Education: Theory and Practice*. He is president of the Network for Change and Continuous Innovation (NCCI)—an organization of colleges and universities from across North America who seek to advance sustainable excellence in higher education by promoting successful practices and approaches used to drive change, innovation, and continuous improvement across academic and administrative functions.